David Garrick, William Wycherley

The Country Wife

A Comedy

David Garrick, William Wycherley

The Country Wife
A Comedy

ISBN/EAN: 9783337069209

Printed in Europe, USA, Canada, Australia, Japan

Cover: Foto ©ninafisch / pixelio.de

More available books at **www.hansebooks.com**

THE
COUNTRY WIFE,

A

COMEDY,

Altered from WYCHERLEY

By DAVID GARRICK, Esq.

Marked with the Variations of the

MANAGER's BOOK,

AT THE

Theatre-Royal in Drury-Lane.

LONDON:
PRINTED FOR C. BATHURST, J. RIVINGTON
AND SONS, T. LONGMAN, T. LOWNDES,
T. CASLON, W. NICOLL, AND S. BLADON.
M.DCC.LXXVII.

ADVERTISEMENT.

THE defire of fhewing * Mifs REYNOLDS to advantage, was the firft motive for attempting an alteration of Wycherley's Country Wife. Tho' near half of the following Play is new written, the Alterer claims no merit, but his endeavour to clear one of our moft celebrated Comedies from immorality and obfcenity. He thought himfelf bound to preferve as much of the original, as could be prefented to an audience of thefe times without offence; and if this Wanton of Charles's days is now fo reclaimed, as to become innocent without being infipid, the prefent Editor will not think his time ill employed, which has enabled him to add fome little variety to the entertainments of the public. There feems indeed an abfolute neceffity for reforming many Plays of our moft eminent writers : for no kind of wit ought to be received as an excufe for immorality, nay it becomes ftill more dangerous in proportion as it is more witty——Without fuch a reformation, our Englifh comedies muft be reduced to a very fmall number, and would pall by a too frequent repetition, or what is worfe, continue fhamelefs in fpite of public difapprobation.

Whatever fate this Play may have in the clofet, it is much indebted to the performers for its favourable reception upon the ftage.

* Who at that time perform'd the part of Peggy, but has fince left the ftage.

Dramatis Personæ.

M E N.

	At Drury Lane.
Moody	Mr. King.
Harcourt	Mr. Palmer.
Sparkish	Mr. Dodd.
Belville	Mr. Cautherly.
Footman	Mr. Wright.
Country Boy	Mr. Burton.

W O M E N.

Alithea	Mrs. Greville.
Miss Peggy	Mrs. Abington.
Lucy	Miss Pope.

SCENE *London.*

THE

COUNTRY WIFE.

ACT I. SCENE Harcourt's *lodgings*.

Harcourt *tying up his stockings, and* Belville *sitting by him.*

Harc. HA, ha, ha! and so you are in love, ne-phew, not reasonably and gallantly, as a young gentleman ought, but sighingly, miserably so—not content to be ankle-deep, you have sous'd over head and ears—ha, Dick?

Belv. I am pretty much in that condition, indeed, uncle. [*Sighs.*

Harc. Nay, never blush at it—when I was of your age I was asham'd too—but three years at college, and half a one at Paris, methinks should have cur'd you of that unfashionable weakness—modesty.

Belv. Could I have releas'd myself from that, I had, perhaps, been at this instant happy in the possession of what I must despair now ever to obtain—Heigho!

Harc. Ha, ha, ha! very foolish indeed.

Belv. Don't laugh at me, uncle; I am foolish, I know; but, like other fools, I deserve to be pitied.

Harc. Prithee don't talk of pity; how can I help you?——for this country girl of yours is certainly married.

Belv. No, no—I won't believe it; she is not married, nor she shan't, if I can help it.

Harc. Well said, modesty—with such a spirit you can help yourself, Dick, without my assistance.

Belv. But you must encourage, and advise me too, or I shall never make any thing of it.

Harc.

Harc. Provided the girl is not married ; for I never, never encourage young men to covet their neighbours wives.

Belv. My heart affures me, that fhe is not married.

Harc. O to be fure, your heart is much to be re-ly'd upon—but to convince you that I have a fellow-feeling of your diftrefs, and that I am as nearly ally'd to you in misfortunes as in relationfhip—you muft know————

Belv. What, uncle ? you alarm me !

Harc. That I am in love too.

Belv. Indeed !

Harc. Miferably in love.'

Belv. That's charming.

Harc. And my miftrefs is juft going to be married to another.

Belv. Better and better.

Harc. I knew my fellow-fufferings would pleafe you; but now prepare for the wonderful wonder-of-wonders !

Belv. Well !————

Harc, My miftrefs is in the fame houfe with yours.

Belv. What, are you in love with Peggy too ?

[Rifing from his chair.

Harc. Well faid, jealoufy.—No, no, fet your heart at reft.—Your Peggy is too young, and too fimple for me.—I muft have one a little more knowing, a little better bred, juft old enough to fee the difference be-tween me and a coxcomb, fpirit enough to break from a brother's engagements, and chufe for herfelf.

Belv. You don't mean Alithea, who is to be married to Mr. Sparkifh ?

Harc. Can't I be in love with a lady that is going to be married to another, as well as you, fir ?

Belv. But Sparkifh is your friend ?

Harc. Prithee don't call him my friend ; he can be nobody's friend, not even his own—He would thruft himfelf into my acquaintance, would introduce me to his miftrefs, tho' I have told him again and again that I was in love with her, which, inftead of

ridding

ridding me of him, has made him only ten times more troublesome—and me really in love—He should suffer for his self-sufficiency.

Belv. 'Tis a conceited puppy!—And what success with the lady?

Harc. No great hopes—and yet, if I could defer the marriage a few days, I should not despair;—her honour, I am confident, is her only attachment to my rival—she can't like Sparkish, and if I can work upon his credulity, a credulity which even popery would be asham'd of, I may yet have the chance of throwing sixes upon the dice to save me.

Belv. Nothing can save me.

Harc. No, not if you whine and sigh, when you should be exerting every thing that is man about you. I have sent Sparkish, who is admitted at all hours in the house, to know how the land lies for you, and if she is not married already.

Belv. How cruel you are—you raise me up with one hand, and then knock me down with the other.

Harc. Well, well, she shan't be married. [*Knocking at the door.*] This is Sparkish, I suppose: don't drop the least hint of your passion to him; if you do, you may as well advertise it in the public papers.

Belv. I'll be careful.

Enter Servant.

Serv. An odd sort of a person, from the country I believe, who calls himself Moody, wants to see you, sir; but as I did not know him, I said you were not at home, but would return directly; *and so will I too,* said he, very short and surly! and away he went, mumbling to himself.

Harc. Very well, Will—I'll see him when he comes. [*Exit Servant.*] Moody call to see me!—He has something more in his head than making me a visit— 'tis to complain of you, I suppose.

Belv. How can he know me?

Harc. We must suppose the worst, and be prepared for him—tell me all you know of this ward of his, this Peggy—Peggy what's her name?

Belv. Thrift, Thrift, uncle.

Harc. Ay, ay, Sir Thomas Thrift's daughter, of Hampſhire, and left very young, under the guardian-ſhip of my old companion and acquaintance, Jack Moody.

Belv. Your companion!—he's old enough to be your father.

Harc. Thank you, nephew—he has greatly the advantage of me in years, as well as wiſdom.—When I firſt launched from the univerſity, into this ocean of London—he was the greateſt rake in it; I knew him well, for near two years, but all of a ſudden he took a freak (a very prudent one) of retiring wholly into the country.

Belv. There he gain'd ſuch an aſcendency over the odd diſpoſition of his neighbour, Sir Thomas, that he left him ſole guardian to his daughter, who forfeits half her fortune, if ſhe does not marry with his conſent—there's the devil, uncle.

Harc. And are you ſo young, ſo fooliſh, and ſo much in love, that you would take her with half her value? ha, nephew?

Belv. I'll take her with any thing—with nothing.

Harc. What! ſuch an unaccompliſh'd, aukward, ſilly creature—he has ſcarce taught her to write—ſhe has ſeen nobody to converſe with, but the country people about 'em; ſo ſhe can do nothing but dangle her arms, look gawky, turn her toes in, and talk broad Hampſhire.

Belv. Don't abuſe her ſweet ſimplicity—had you but heard her talk, as I have done, from the garden-wall in the country, by moon-light——

Harc. Romeo and Juliet, I proteſt, ha, ha, ha! *Ariſe fair ſun, and kill the envious*——ha, ha, ha! How often have you ſeen this fair Capulet?

Belv. I ſaw her three times in the country, and ſpoke to her twice; I have leap'd an orchard-wall, like Romeo, to come at her, play'd the balcony-ſcene, from an old ſummer-houſe in the garden; and if I loſe her, I will find out an apothecary, and play the tomb-ſcene too, for I cannot bear to be croſs'd in love.

Harc. Well ſaid, Dick!—this ſpirit muſt produce
ſomething

fomething—but has the old dragon ever caught you fighing at her?

Belv. Never in the country; he faw me yefterday kiffing my hand to her, from the new tavern-window that looks upon the back of his houfe, and immediately drove her from it, and faften'd up the window-fhutters. [*Sparkifh without.*

Spark. Very well, Will, I'll go up to 'em.

Harc. I hear Sparkifh coming up—take care of what I told you—not a word of Peggy;—hear his intelligence, and make ufe of it, without feeming to mind it.

Belv. Mum, mum, uncle.

Enter Sparkifh.

Spark. O, my dear Harcourt, I fhall die with laughing—I have fuch news for thee—ha, ha, ha!— What, your nephew too, and a little dumpifh, or fo —you have been giving him a lecture upon œconomy, I fuppofe—you, who never had any, can beft defcribe the evils that arife from the want of it.—I never mind my own affairs, not I.—I hear, Mr. Belville, you have got a pretty fnug houfe, with a bow-window that looks into the park, and a back-door that goes out into it.—Very convenient, and well-imagin'd— no young, handfome fellow fhould be without one— you may be always ready there, like a fpider in his web, to feize upon ftray'd women of quality.

Harc. As you us'd to do—you vain fellow you; prithee don't teach my nephew your abandoned tricks —he is a modeft young man, and you muft not fpoil him.—

Spark. May be fo; but his modefty has done fome mifchief at our houfe—my furly, jealous brother-in-law faw that modeft young gentleman cafting a wifh-ful eye at his forbidden fruit, from the new tavern-window.

Belv. You miftake the perfon, Mr. Sparkifh—I don't know what young lady you mean.

Harc. Explain yourfelf, Sparkifh, you muft mi-ftake—Dick has never feen the girl.

Spark. I don't fay he has; I only tell you what Moody fays. Befides, he went to the tavern himfelf,

A and

and enquir'd of the waiter, who din'd in the back-room,—No. 4 —and they told him it was Mr. Belville, your nephew—that's all I know of the matter, or defire to know of it—faith.

Harc. He kifs'd his hand, indeed, to your lady, Alithea, and is more in love with her than you are, and very near as much as I am ; fo look about you, fuch a youth may be dangerous.

Spark. The more danger the more honour : I defy you both—win her and wear her, if you can—*Dolus an virtus* in love as well as in war—tho' you muft be expeditious, faith ; for I believe, if I don't change my mind, I fhall marry her to-morrow, or the day after. —Have you no honeft clergyman, Harcourt, no fellow-collegian to recommend to me to do the bufinefs ?

Harc. Nothing ever, fure, was fo lucky. [*Afide.*] Why, faith, I have, Sparkifh—my brother, a twin-brother, Ned Harcourt, will be in town to-day, and proud to attend your commands.—I am a very generous rival, you fee, to lend you my brother to marry the woman I love !

Spark. And fo am I too, to let your brother come fo near us—but Ned fhall be the man ; poor Alithea grows impatient—I can't put off the evil day any longer—I fancy the brute, her brother, has a mind to marry his country idiot at the fame time.

Belv. How, country idiot, fir !

Harc. Taifez vous bête. [*Afide to* Belv.] I thought he had been married already.

Spark. No, no, he's not married, that's the joke of it.

Belv. No, no, he is not married.

Harc. Hold your tongue—   [*Elbowing* Belville.

Spark. Not he—I have the fineft ftory to tell you— by the by, he intends calling upon you, for he afk'd me where you liv'd, to complain of *modefty* there— He pick'd up an old raking acquaintance of his, as we came along together—Will. Frankly, who faw him with his girl, fculking and muffled up, at the play laft night—he plagu'd him much about matrimony,

mony, and his being afham'd to fhew himfelf; fwore
he was in love with his wife, and intended to cuckold
him. Do you? cry'd Moody, folding his arms, and
fcowling with his eyes thus — *You muſt have more wit
than you us'd to have — Befides, if you have as much as
you think you have, I ſhall be out of your reach, and this
profligate metropolis, in leſs than a week.* — Moody
would fain have got rid of him, but the other held
him by the ſleeve, ſo I left 'em ; rejoiced moſt luxu-
riouſly to ſee the poor devil tormented.

Belv. I thought you ſaid, juſt now, that he was *not*
married — is not that a contradiction, ſir ?

[Harcourt *ſtill makes ſigns to* Belville.

Spark. Why, it is a kind of one — but confidering
your modeſty, and your ignorance of the young lady,
you are pretty tolerably inquiſitive, methinks, ha,
Harcourt ! ha, ha, ha !

Harc. Pooh, pooh !. don't talk to that baby, tell
me all you know.

Spark. You muſt know, my booby of a brother-in-
law hath brought up this ward of his (a good fortune
let me tell you) as he coops up and fattens his
chickens, for his own eating — he is plaguy jealous of
her, and was very ſorry that he could not marry her in
the country, without coming up to town ; which he
could not do, on account of ſome writings or other ;
ſo what does my gentleman? he perfuades the poor
filly girl, by breaking a ſix-pence, or ſome non-
fenſe or another, that they are to all intents married
in heaven ; but that the laws require the ſigning of
articles, and the church-ſervice to complete their
union — ſo he has made her call him huſband, and
Bud, which ſhe conſtantly does, and he calls her wife,
and gives out ſhe is married, that ſhe may not look
after younger fellows, nor younger fellows after her,
egad ; ha, ha, ha ! and all won't do.

Belv. Thank you, ſir —— what heav'nly news,
uncle !

Harc. What an idiot you are, nephew ! And ſo
then you make but one trouble of it; and are both
to be tack'd together the ſame day?

A. 6 *Spark.*

Spark. No, no, he can't be married this week; he damns the lawyers for keeping him in town ;—— befides, I am out of favour; and he is continually fnarling at me, and abufing me, for not being jealous. [*Knocking at the door.*] There he is—I muſt not be feen with you, for he'll fufpeċt fomething; I'll go with your nephew to his houfe, and we'll wait for you, and make a viſit to my wife that is to be, and, perhaps, we ſhall ſhew young modeſty here a ſight of Peggy too.

Enter Servant.

Serv. Sir, here's the ſtrange odd fort of a gentleman come again, and I have ſhewn him into the fore-parlour.

Spark. That muſt be Moody! well faid, Will; an odd fort of a ſtrange gentleman indeed; we'll ſtep into the next room 'till he comes into this, and then you may have him all to yourfelf—much good may do you. [Sparkiſh *going, returns.*] Remember that he is married, or he'll fufpeċt me of betraying him.

[*Ex.* Sparkiſh *and* Belville.

Harc. Shew him up, Will. [*Exit* Serv.] Now muſt I prepare myfelf to fee a very ſtrange, tho' a very natural metamorphoſis—a once high-ſpirited, handſome, well-drefs'd, raking prodigal of the town, funk into a furly, fufpicious, œconomical, country ſloven —— le voilà.

Enter Moody.

Mood. Mr. Harcourt, your humble fervant—have you forgot me?

Harc. What, my old friend Jack Moody! by thy long abfence from the town, the grumnefs of thy countenance, and the ſlovenlinefs of thy habit, I ſhould give thee joy—you are certainly married.

Moody. My long ſtay in the country will excufe my drefs, and I have a fuit at law that brings me up to town, and puts me out of humour—befides, I muſt give Sparkiſh ten thoufand pounds to-morrow to take my fiſter off my hands.

Harc. Your fiſter is very much obliged to you—— being fo much older than her, you have taken upon
you

you the authority of a father, and have engaged her to a coxcomb.

Moody. I have, and to oblige her——nothing but coxcombs or debauchees are the favourites now-a-days, and a coxcomb is rather the more innocent animal of the two.

Harc. She has fenfe, and tafte, and can't like him; fo you muft anfwer for the confequences.

Moody. When fhe is out of my hands, her hufband muft look to confequences. He's a fafhionable fool, and will cut his horns kindly.

Harc. And what is to fecure your worfhip from confequences ?—I did not expeft marriage from fuch a rake——one that knew the town fo well : fye, fye, Jack.

Moody. I'll tell you my fecurity—I have married no London wife.

Harc. That's all one—that grave circumfpeftion in marrying a country wife, is like refufing a deceitful, pamper'd, Smithfield jade, to go and be cheated by a friend in the country.

Moody. I wifh the devil had both him and his fimile.
                                                    [*Afide.*

Harc. Well, never grumble about it, what's done can't be undone ; is your wife handfome, and young ?

Moody. She has little beauty but her youth, nothing to brag of but her health, and no attraftion but her modefty——wholfome, homely, and houfewifely—that's all.

Harc. You talk as like a grazier as you look, Jack —why did you not bring her to town before, to be taught fomething ?

Moody. Which fomething I might repent as long as I live-—No, no ; women and private foldiers fhould be ignorant.

Harc. But, prithee, why wouldft thou marry her, if fhe be ugly, ill-bred, and filly ? She muft be rich then.

Moody. As rich as if fhe had the wealth of the Mogul —fhe'll not ruin her hufband, like a London-baggage, with a million of vices fhe never heard of—then, be-
                                                    caufe

caufe fhe's ugly, fhe's the likelier to be my own ; and being ill-bred, fhe'll hate converfation ; and fince filly and innocent, will not know the difference between me and you ; that is, between a man of thirty, and one of forty.

Harc. Fifty, to my knowledge—[Moody *turns off, and grumbles.*]—But fee how you and I differ, Jack— wit to me is more neceffary than beauty : I think no young woman ugly that has it ; and no handfome woman agreeable without it.

Moody. 'Tis my maxim—He's a fool that marries ; but he's a greater that does not marry a fool.——I know the town, Mr. Harcourt ; and my wife fhall be virtuous in fpite of you, or your nephew.

Harc. My nephew !—poor fheepifh lad—he runs away from every woman he fees—he faw your fifter Alithea at the opera, and was much fmitten with her —He always toafts her—and hates the very name of Sparkifh. I'll bring him to your houfe——and you fhall fee what a formidable Tarquin he is.

Moody. I have no curiofity, fo give yourfelf no trouble.——You have heard of a wolf in fheep's cloathing, and I have feen your innocent nephew kiffing his hands at my windows.

Harc. At your fifter, I fuppofe ; nor at her unlefs he was tipfy —How can you, Jack, be fo outrageoufly fufpicious ? Sparkifh has promis'd to introduce him to his miftrefs.

Moody. Sparkifh is a fool, and may be, what I'll take care not to be ——I confefs my vifit to you, Mr. Harcourt, was partly for old acquaintance fake, but chiefly to defire your nephew to confine his gallantries to the tavern, and not fend 'em in looks, figns, or tokens, on the other fide the way—I keep no brothel—fo pray tell your nephew. [*Going.*

Harc. Nay, prithee, Jack, leave me in better humour—Well, I'll tell him, ha, ha, ha ! poor Dick, how he'll ftare. This will give him a reputation, and the girls won't laugh at him any longer. Shall we dine together at the tavern, and fend for my nephew to chide him for his gallantry ? Ha, ha, ha ! we fhall have fine fport.

6

Moody.

Moody. I am not to be laugh'd out of my fenfes,
Mr. Harcourt——I was once a modeft, meek, young
gentleman myfelf, and I never have been half fo mif-
chievous before or fince, as I was in that ftate of innocence.—And fo, old friend, make no ceremony with
me—I have much bufinefs, and you have much pleafure, and therefore, as I hate forms, I will excufe
your returning my vifit ; or fending your nephew to
fatisfy me of his modefty—and fo your fervant. [*Exit.*

Harc. Ha, ha, ha! poor Jack! what a life of
fufpicion does he lead ! I pity the poor fellow, tho'
he ought, and will fuffer for his folly——Folly !—'tis
treafon, murder, facrilege! When perfons of a cer-
tain age will indulge their falfe ungenerous appetites,
at the expence of a young creature's happinefs, dame
Nature will revenge herfelf upon them, for thwarting
her moft heavenly will and pleafure. [*Exit.*

ACT II. SCENE *a chamber in* Moody's *houfe.*

Enter Mifs Peggy *and* Alithea.

Peg. PRAY, fifter, where are the beft fields and
woods to walk in, in London ?

Alith. A pretty queftion ! why, fifter, Vauxhall,
Ranelagh, and St. James's Park, are the moft fre-
quented.

Peg. Pray, fifter, tell me why my Bud looks fo
grum here in town, and keeps me up clofe, and will
not let me go a walking, nor let me wear my beft
gown yefterday.

Alith. O, he's jealous, fifter.

Peg. Jealous ! what's that ?

Alith. He's afraid you fhould love another man.

Peg. How fhould he be afraid of my loving another man, when he will not let me fee any but himfelf ?

Alith. Did he not carry you yefterday to a play ?

Peg. Ay ; but we fat amongft ugly people : he
would

would not let me come near the gentry, who fat under us, fo that I could not fee 'em. He told me none but naughty women fat there—but I would have ventur'd for all that.

Alith. But how did you like the play?

Peg. Indeed I was weary of the play; but I lik'd hugeoufly the actors; they are the goodlieft, propereft men, fifter.

Alith. O, but you muft not like the actors, fifter.

Peg. Ay, how fhould I help it, fifter? Pray, fifter, when my guardian comes in, will you afk leave for me to go a walking?

Alith. A walking, ha, ha, ha! Lord, a country gentlewoman's pleafure is the drudgery of a foot-poft; and fhe requires as much airing as her hufband's horfes. [*Afide.*] [*Enter* Moody.] But here comes my brother, I'll afk him, tho' I'm fure he'll not grant it.

Peg. O my dear, dear Bud, welcome home; why doft thou look fo fropifh? who has nanger'd thee?

Moody. You're a fool. [Peggy *goes afide, and cries.*

Alith. Faith, and fo fhe is, for crying for no fault —poor tender creature!

Moody. What, you would have her as impudent as yourfelf, as arrant a gilflirt, a gadder, a magpye, and, to fay all, a mere notorious town-woman!

Alith. Brother, you are my only cenfurer; and the honour of your family will fooner fuffer in your wife that is to be, than in me, tho' I take the innocent liberty of the town!

Moody. Hark you, miftrefs, do not talk fo before my wife: the innocent liberty of the town!

Alith. Pray what ill people frequent my lodgings? I keep no company with any woman of fcandalous reputation.

Moody. No, you keep the men of fcandalous reputation company.

Alith. Would you not have me civil, anfwer 'em at public places, walk with 'em when they join me in the Park, Ranelagh, or Vauxhall?

Moody. Hold, hold; do not teach my wife where

3   the

the men are to be found: I believe she's the worse for
your town documents already. I bid you keep her in
ignorance, as I do.

Peg. Indeed, be not angry with her, Bud, she will
tell me nothing of the town, tho' I ask her a thousand
times a day.

Moody. Then you are very inquisitive to know, I
find ?

Peg. Not I, indeed, dear ; I hate London : our
place-house in the country is worth a thousand of 't ;
would I were there again !

Moody. So you shall, I warrant. But were you
not talking of plays and players when I came in ? you
are her encourager in such discourses.

Peg. No, indeed, dear; she chid me just now for
liking the player-men.

Moody. Nay, if she is so innocent as to own to me
her liking them, there is no hurt in't. [*Aside.*] Come,
my poor rogue, but thou likest none better than
me ?

Peg. Yes, indeed, but I do ; the player-men are
finer folks.

Moody. But you love none better than me ?

Peg. You are my own dear Bud, and I know you ;
I hate strangers.

Moody. Ay, my dear, you must love me only ; and
not be like the naughty town-women, who only hate
their husbands, and love every man else ; love plays,
visits, fine coaches, fine cloaths, fiddles, balls, treats,
and so lead a wicked town-life.

Peg. Nay, if to enjoy all these things be a town-
life, London is not so bad a place, dear.

Moody. How ! if you love me, you must hate London.

Alith. The fool has forbid me discovering to her
the pleasures of the town, and he is now setting her
agog upon them himself. [*Aside.*

Peg. But, Bud, do the town-women love the player-
men too ?

Moody. Yes, I warrant you.

Peg. Ay, I warrant you.

Moody.

Moody. Why, you do not, I hope ?

Peg. No, no, Bud ; but why have we no player-men in the country ?

Moody. Ha ! Mrs. Minx, aſk me no more to go to a play.

Peg. Nay, why, love ? I did not care for going : but when you forbid me, you make me as 'twere deſire it.

Alith. So 'twill be in other things, I warrant. [*Aſide.*

Peg. Pray let me go to a play, dear ?

Moody. Hold your peace, I won't.

Peg. Why, love ?

Moody. Why, I'll tell you.

Alith. Nay, if he tell her, ſhe'll give him more cauſe to forbid her that place. [*Aſide.*

Peg. Pray, why, dear ?

Moody. Firſt, you like the actors ; and the gallants may like you.

Peg. What, a homely country girl ? No, Bud, nobody will like me.

Moody. I tell you yes, they may.

Peg. No, no, you jeſt—I won't believe you : I will go.

Moody. I tell you then, that one of the moſt raking fellows in town, who ſaw you there, told me he was in love with you.

Peg. Indeed ! who, who, pray, who was't ?

Moody. I've gone too far, and ſlipt before I was aware, How overjoy'd ſhe is ! [*Aſide.*

Peg. Was it any Hampſhire gallant, any of our neighbours ?——Promiſe you I am beholden to him.

Moody. I promiſe you, you lye ; for he wou'd but ruin you, as he has done hundreds.

Peg. Ay, but if he loves me, why ſhould he ruin me ? anſwer me to that. Methinks he ſhou'd not ; I wou'd do him no harm.

Alith. Ha, ha, ha !

Moody. 'Tis very well ; but I'll keep him from doing you any harm, or me either. But here comes company, get you in, get you in.

Peg.

Peg. But pray, husband, is he a pretty gentleman that loves me?

Moody. In, baggage, in.

[*Thrusts her in, and shuts the door.*

. *Enter* Sparkish, Harcourt, *and* Belville.

Moody. What, all the libertines of the town brought to my lodging, by this easy coxcomb! 'Sdeath, I'll not suffer it.

Spark. Here, Belville, do you approve my choice? Dear little rogue, I told you, I'd bring you acquainted with all my friends, the wits.

Moody. Ay, they shall know her as well as you yourself will, I warrant you.

Spark. This is one of those, my pretty rogue, that are to dance at your wedding to-morrow. And one you must make welcome, for he's modest. [Belville *salutes* Alithea.] Harcourt makes himself welcome, and has not the same foible, though of the same. family.

Harc. You are too obliging, Sparkish.

Moody. And so he is indeed—the fop's horns will as naturally sprout upon his brows, as mushrooms upon dunghills.

Harc. This, Mr. Moody, is my nephew you mentioned to me; I would bring him with me, for a sight of him will be sufficient, without poppy or mandragora, to restore you to your rest.

Belv. I am sorry, sir, that any mistake or imprudence of mine, should have given you any uneasiness; it was not so intended, I assure you, sir.

Moody. It may be so, sir, but not the less criminal for that—My wife, sir, must not be smirk'd and nodded at from tavern windows; I am a good shot, young gentleman, and don't suffer magpies to come near my cherries.

Belv. Was it your wife, sir?

Moody. What's that to you, sir—suppose it was my grandmother?

. *Belv.* I would not dare to offend her—permit me to say a word in private to you.

[Moody *and* Belville *retire out of sight.*

Spark.

Spark. Now old furly is gone, tell me, Harcourt, if thou lik'ft her as well as ever—My dear, don't look down, I fhould hate to have a wife of mine out of countenance at any thing.

Alith. For fhame, Mr. Sparkifh.

Spark. Tell me, I fay, Harcourt, how doft like her? thou haft ftar'd upon her enough to refolve me.

Harc. So infinitely well, that I could wifh I had a miftrefs too, that might differ from her in nothing but her love and engagement to you.

Alith. Sir, Mr. Sparkifh has often told me, that his acquaintance were all wits and railers, and now I find it.

Spark. No, by the univerfe, madam, he does not rally now; you may believe him; I do affure you he is the honefteft, worthieft, true-hearted gentleman; a man of fuch perfect honour, he would fay nothing to a lady he does not mean.

Harc. Sir, you are fo beyond expectation obliging, that——

Spark. Nay, egad, I am fure you do admire her extremely, I fee it in your eyes—He does admire you, madam, he has told me fo a thoufand and a thoufand times—have you not, Harcourt? You do admire her, by the world you do—don't you?

Harc. Yes, above the world, or the moft glorious part of it, her whole fex; and 'till now, I never thought I fhould have envied you or any man about to marry: but you have the beft excufe to marry I ever knew.

Alith. Nay, now, fir, I am fatisfied you are of the fociety of the wits and railers, fince you cannot fpare your friend, even when he is moft civil to you; but the fureft fign is, you are an enemy to marriage, the common butt of every railer.

Harc. Truly, madam, I was never an enemy to marriage till now, becaufe marriage was never an enemy to me before.

Alith. But why, fir, is marriage an enemy to you now? becaufe it robs you of your friend here? for you look upon a friend married, as one gone into a monaftery, that is dead to the world.

Harc.

Harc. 'Tis indeed, because you marry him; I see, madam, you can guess my meaning: I do confess heartily and openly, I wish it were in my power to break the match; by Heav'ns I wou'd.

Spark. Poor Frank!

Alith. Wou'd you be so unkind to me?

Harc. No, no, 'tis not because I wou'd be unkind to you.

Spark. Poor Frank; no, egad, 'tis only his kindness to me.

Alith. Great kindness to you indeed!—Insensible! Let a man make love to his mistress to his face.   [*Aside.*

Spark. Come, dear Frank, for all my wife there, that shall be, thou shalt enjoy me sometimes, dear rogue: by my honour, we men of wit condole for our deceased brother in marriage, as much as for one dead in earnest: I think that was prettily said of me, ha, Harcourt?——But come, Frank, be not melancholy for me.

Harc. No, I assure you, I am not melancholy for you.

Spark. Prithee, Frank, dost think my wife, that shall be, there, a fine person?

Harc. I cou'd gaze upon her, till I became as blind as you are.

Spark. How, as I am? how?

Harc. Because you are a lover; and true lovers are blind, stock blind.

Spark. True, true; but by the world she has wit too, as well as beauty; go, go with her into a corner, and try if she has wit; talk to her any thing, she's bashful before me.

Alith. Sir, you dispose of me a little before your time.   [*Aside to* Sparkish.

Spark. Nay, nay, madam, let me have an earnest of your obedience, or—go, go, madam.

       [Harcourt *courts* Alithea *aside.*

Enter Moody.

Moody. How, sir, if you are not concern'd for the honour of a wife, I am for that of a sister;—be a pander
           der

der to your own wife, bring men to her, let 'em make
love before your face, thruſt 'em into a corner together, then leave 'em in private! is this your town
wit and conduct?

Spark. Ha, ha, ha! a ſilly wife rogue wou'd make
one laugh more than a ſtark fool : ha, ha, ha! I ſhall
burſt. Nay, you ſhall not diſturb 'em ; I'll vex thee,
by the world. What have you done with Belville?
　　　[*Struggles with* Moody, *to keep him from* Har-
　　　court *and* Alithea.

Moody. Shewn him the way out of my houſe, as
you ſhould to that gentleman.

Spark. Nay, but prithee—let me reaſon with thee.
　　　　　　　[*Talks apart with* Moody.

Alith. The writings are drawn, ſir, ſettlements
made ; 'tis too late, ſir, and paſt all revocation.

Harc. Then ſo is my death.

Alith. I wou'd not be unjuſt to him.

Harc. Then why to me ſo?

Alith. I have no obligations to you.

Harc. My love.

Alith. I had his before.

Harc. You never had it; he wants, you ſee, jea-
louſy, the only infallible ſign of it.

Alith. Love proceeds from eſteem ; he cannot diſ-
truſt my virtue ; beſides, he loves me, or he wou'd
not marry me.

Harc. Marrying you is no more a ſign of his love,
than bribing your woman that he may marry you, is
a ſign of his generoſity. But if you take marriage
for a ſign of love, take it from me immediately.

Alith. No, now you have put a ſcruple in my head :
but in ſhort, ſir, to end our diſpute, I muſt marry
him ; my reputation wou'd ſuffer in the world elſe.

Harc. No ; if you do marry him, with your pardon, madam, your reputation ſuffers in the world.

Alith. Nay, now you are rude, ſir—Mr. Sparkiſh,
pray come hither, your friend here is very trouble-
ſome, and very loving.

Harc. Hold, hold. 　　　　[*Aſide to* Alithea.

Moody. D'ye hear that, ſenſeleſs puppy?

　　　　　　　　　　　　　　　Spark.

Spark. Why, d'ye think I'll feem jealous, like a country bumpkin?

Moody. No, rather be difhonour'd, like a credulous driv'ler.

Harc. Madam, you would not have been fo little generous as to have told him?

Alith. Yes, fince you cou'd be fo little generous as to wrong him.

Harc. Wrong him! no man can do't, he's beneath an injury; a bubble, a coward, a fenfelefs idiot, a wretch fo contemptible to all the world but you, that ————

Alith. Hold, do not rail at him; for fince he is like to be my hufband, I am refolv'd to like him: nay, I think I am oblig'd to tell him, you are not his friend.—Mr. Sparkifh, Mr. Sparkifh!

Spark. What, what; now dear rogue, has not fhe wit?

Harc. Not fo much as I thought, and hoped fhe had.   [*Surlily.*

Alith. Mr. Sparkifh, do you bring people to rail at you?

Harc. Madam!

Spark. How! no; but if he does rail at me, 'tis but in jeft, I warrant: what we wits do for one another, and never take any notice of it.

Alith. He fpoke fo fcurriloufly of you, I had no patience to hear him.

Moody. And he was in the right on't.

Alith. Befides, he has been making love to me.

Moody. And I told the fool fo.

Harc. True, damn'd tell-tale woman.   [*Afide.*

Spark. Pfhaw, to fhew his parts—We wits rail and make love often, but to fhew our parts; as we have no affections, fo we have no malice, we————

Moody. Did you ever hear fuch an afs!

Alith. He faid you were a wretch, below an injury.

Spark. Pfhaw.

Harc. Madam!

Alith. A common bubble.

Spark.

Spark. Pſhaw. /

Alith. A coward !

Spark. Pſhaw, pſhaw !

Alith. A ſenſeleſs drivelling idiot.

Moody. True, true, true ; all true.

Spark. How! did he diſparage my parts? nay, then my honour's concern'd. I can't put up that, ſir; by the world, brother, help me to kill him.

[*Offers to draw.*

Alith. Hold, hold.

Spark. What, what?

Alith. I muſt not let 'em kill the gentleman, neiⁱ ther.   [*Aſide.*

Spark. I'll be thy death.   [*Putting up his ſword.*

Moody. If Harcourt would but kill Sparkiſh, and run away with my ſiſter, I ſhou'd be rid of three plagues at once.

Alith. ' Hold, hold;' indeed, to tell the truth, the gentleman ſaid, after all, that what he ſpoke was but out of friendſhip to you.

Spark. How! ſay I am a fool, that is no wit, out of friendſhip to me?

Alith. Yes, to try whether I was concern'd enough for you ; and made love to me only to be ſatisfy'd of my virtue, for your ſake.

Harc. Kind, however!   [*Aſide.*

Spark. Nay, if it were ſo, my dear rogue, I aſk thee pardon ; but why wou'd not you tell me ſo, faith?

Harc. Becauſe I did not think on't, faith !

Spark. Come, Belville is gone away ; Harcourt, let's be gone to the new play—Come, madam.

Alith. I will not go, if you intend to leave me alone in the box, and run all about the houſe, as you uſe to do.

Spark. Pſhaw, I'll leave Harcourt with you in the box, to entertain you, and that's as good ; if I ſat in the box, I ſhou'd be thought no critic—I muſt run about, my dear, and abuſe the author—Come away, Harcourt, lead her down. B'ye, brother.

[*Ex.* Harcourt, Sparkiſh, *and* Alithea.

Moody. B'ye, driv'ler. Well, go thy ways, for the
flower

flower of the true town fops, fuch as fpend their eftates before they come to 'em, and are cuckolds before they're married. But let me go look to my freehold.

Enter a Servant Boy.

Boy. Mafter, your worfhip's fervant—here is the lawyer, counfeller gentleman, with a green bag full of papers, come again, and would be glad to fpeak to you.

Moody. Now here's fome other damn'd impediment, which the law has ·hrown in our way——I fhall never marry the girl, nor get clear of the fmoke and wickednefs of this curfed town. Where is he?

Boy. He's below in a coach, with three other lawyer, counfeller gentlemen. [*Exeunt*.

S C E N E *changes*.

Enter Mifs Peggy *and* Lucy.

Lucy. What ails you, Mifs Peggy? you are grown quite melancholy.

Peg. Would it not make any one melancholy to fee your miftrefs Alithea go every day fluttering about abroad to plays and affemblies, and I know not what, whilft I muft ftay at home, like a poor lonely fullen bird in a cage?

Lucy. Dear mifs Peggy, I thought you chofe to be confin'd: I imagin'd that you had been bred fo young to the cage, that you had no pleafure in flying about, and hopping in the open air, as other young ladies, who go a little wild about this town.

Peg. Nay, I confefs I was quiet enough, till fomebody told me what pure lives the London ladies lead, with their dancing-meetings, and junketings, and drefs'd every day in their beft gowns; and I warrant you play at nine-pins every day in the week, fo they do.

Lucy. To be fure, mifs, you will lead a better life when join'd in holy wedlock with your fweet-temper'd guardian, the chearful Mr. Moody.

Peg. I can't lead a worfe, that's one good thing— but I muft make the beft of a bad market, for I can't marry nobody elfe.

Lucy. How fo, mifs? that's very ftrange.

B   *Peg.*

Peg. Why we have a contraction to one another—
fo we are as good as married, you know——

Lucy. I know it! Heav'n forbid, mifs——

Peg. Heigho!

Lucy. Don't figh, mifs Peggy—if that young gentleman, who was here juft now, would take pity on
me, I'd throw fuch a contract as yours behind the
fire.

Peg. Lord blefs us, how you talk!

Lucy. Young Mr. Belville wou'd make you talk
otherwife, if you knew him.

Peg. Mr. Belville!—where is he?—when did you
fee him?—you have undone me, Lucy—where was
he? did he fay any thing?

Lucy. Say any thing! very little, indeed—he's
quite diftracted, poor young creature. He was talking with your guardian juft now.

Peg. The deuce he was!—but where was it, and
when was it?—

Lucy. In this houfe, five minutes ago, when your
guardian turn'd you into your chamber, for fear of
your being feen.

Peg. I knew fomething was the matter, I was in
fuch a flufter —.But what did he fay to my Bud?

Lucy. What do you call him Bud for? Bud means
hufband, and he is not your hufband yet—and I hope
never will be—and if he was my hufband, I'd bud
him, a furly unreafonable beaft.

Peg. I'd call him any names, to keep him in good
humour—if he'd let me marry any body elfe, (which
I can't do) I'd call him hufband as long as he liv'd—
But what faid Mr. Belville to him?

Lucy. I don't know what he faid to him, but I'll
tell you what he faid to me, with a figh, and his
hand upon his breaft as he went out of the door—If
you ever were in love, young gentlewoman, (meaning
me) and can pity a moft faithful lover—tell the dear
object of my affections————

Peg. Meaning me, Lucy?

Lucy. Yes, you, to be fure. Tell the dear object
of my affections, I live but upon the hopes that fhe

is not married; and when thofe hopes leave me——
fhe knows the reft——then he caft up his eyes thus—
gnafh'd his teeth—ftruck his forehead—would have
fpoke again, but could not—fetch'd a deep figh, and
vanifh'd.

Peg. 'That is really very fine—I'm fure it makes
my heart fink within me, and brings tears into my
eyes—O he's a charming fweet—but hufh, hufh, I
hear my hufband!

Lucy. Don't call him hufband. Go into the Park
this evening if you can.

Peg. Mum, mum——

Enter Moody.

Moody. Come, what's here to do? you are putting
the town pleafures in her head, and fetting her a
longing.

Lucy. Yes, after nine-pins; you fuffer none to
give her thofe longings you mean, but yourfelf.

Moody. Come, Mrs. Flippant, good precepts are
loft when bad examples are ftill before us: the liberty
your miftrefs takes abroad makes her hanker after it,
and out of humour at home: poor wretch! fhe defired not to come to London; I would bring her.

Lucy. O yes, you furfeit her with pleafures.

Moody. She has been this fortnight in town, and
never defired, till this afternoon, to go abroad.

Lucy. Was fhe not at the play yefterday?

Moody. Yes, but fhe never afk'd me: I was myfelf
the caufe of her going.

Lucy. Then if fhe afk you again, you are the
caufe of her afking, and not my miftrefs.

Moody. Well, next week I fhall be rid of you all,
rid of this town, and my dreadful apprehenfions.
Come, be not melancholy, for thou fhalt go into the
country very foon, deareft.

Lucy. Great comfort!

Peg. Pifh! what d'ye tell me of the country for?

Moody. How's this! what, pifh at the country?

Peg. Let me alone, I am not well.

Moody. O, if that be all—what ails my deareft?

Peg. Truly, I don't know; but I have not been

well

well fince you told me there was a gallant at the play
in love with me.

Moody. Ha!

Lucy. That's my miftrefs too.

Moody. Nay, if you are not well, but are fo concern'd becaufe a raking fellow chanced to lye, and fay
he lik'd you, you'll make me fick too.

Peg. Of what ficknefs?

Moody. O, of that which is worfe than the plague,
jealoufy.

Peg. Pifh, you jeer: I'm fure there's no fuch dif-
eafe in our receipt-book at home.

Moody. No, thou never met with it, poor innocent.

Peg. Well, but pray, Bud, let's go to a play to-
night.

Moody. No, no;—no more plays—But why are you
fo eager to fee a play?

Peg. Faith, dear, not that I care one pin for their
talk there; but I like to look upon the player-men,
and wou'd fee, if I could, the gallant you fay loves
me: that's all, dear Bud.

Moody. Is that all, dear Bud?

Lucy. This proceeds from my miftrefs's example.

Peg. Let's go abroad, however, dear Bud, if we
don't go to the play.

Moody. Come, have a little patience, and thou fhalt
go into the country next week.

Peg. Therefore I would fee firft fome fights, to
tell my neighbours of: nay, I will go abroad, that's
once.

Moody. What, you have put this into her head?

Lucy. Heav'n defend me, what fufpicions! fomebody has put more things into your head than you ought
to have.

Moody. Your tongue runs too glibly, madam, and
you have liv'd too long with a London lady, to be
a proper companion for innocence—I am not over-
fond of your miftrefs.

Lucy. There's no love loft between us.

Moody. You admitted thofe gentlemen into the

houfe,

houfe, when I faid I wou'd not be at home; and there was the young fellow too who behav'd fo indecently to my wife at the tavern-window.

Lucy. Becaufe you wou'd not let him fee your hand-fome wife out of your lodgings.

Peg. Why, O Lord! did the gentleman come hi-ther to fee me indeed?

Moody. No, no, you are not the caufe of that damn'd queftion too.

Peg. Come, pray, Bud, let's go abroad before 'tis late; for I will go, that's flat and plain—only into the park.

Moody. So! the obftinacy already of the town-wife; and I muft, whilft fhe's here, humour her like one. [*Afide.*] How fhall we do, that fhe may not be feen or known?

Lucy. Muffle her up with a bonnet and handker-chief, and I'll go with her to avoid fufpicion.

Moody. ' And run into more danger.'—No, no, I am obliged to you for your kindnefs, but fhe fhan't ftir without me.

Lucy. What will you do then?

Peg. What, fhall we go? I am fick with ftaying at home: if I don't walk in the park, I'll do nothing that I am bid for a week—I won't be mop'd.

Lucy. O, fhe has a charming fpirit! I could ftand your friend now, and would, if you had ever a civil word to give me.

Moody. I'll give thee a better thing, I'll give thee a guinea for thy good advice, if I like it; and I can have the beft of the college for the fame money.

Lucy. I defpife a bribe—when I am your friend, it fhall be without fee or reward.

Peg. Don't be long then, for I will go out.

Lucy. The taylor brought home laft night the clothes you intend for a prefent to your godfon in the country.

Peg. You muft not tell that, Lucy.

Lucy. But I will, madam—When you were with your lawyers laft night, Mifs Peggy, to divert me and herfelf, put 'em on, and they fitted her to a hair.

Moody.

Moody. Thank you, thank you, Lucy, 'tis the luckieſt thought! Go this moment, Peggy, into your chamber, and put 'em on again—and you ſhall walk with me into the park, as my godſon—Well thought of, Lucy—I ſhall love you for ever for this.

Peg. And ſo ſhall I too, Lucy, I'll put 'em on directly. [*Going, returns.*] Suppoſe, Bud, I muſt keep on my petticoats, for fear of ſhewing my legs?

Moody. No, no, you fool, never mind your legs.

Peg. No more I will then, Bud——This is pure.
[*Exit rejoiced.*

Moody. What a ſimpleton it is! Well, Lucy, I thank you for the thought, and before I leave London, thou ſhalt be convinc'd how much I am obliged to thee. [*Exit ſmiling.*

Lucy. And before you leave London, Mr. Moody, I hope I ſhall convince you how much you are oblig'd to me. [*Exit.*

ACT III. SCENE *the park.*

Enter Belville, *and* Harcourt.

Belv. AND the moment Moody left me, and before I left his lodgings, I took an opportunity of conveying ſome tender ſentiments thro' Lucy to Miſs Peggy, and it was Lucy advis'd me to ſtrole here this evening;—and here I am, in expectation of ſeeing my country goddeſs.

Harc. And ſo to blind Moody, and take him off the ſcent of your paſſion for this girl, and at the ſame time, to give me an opportunity with Sparkiſh's miſtreſs, (and of which I have made the moſt) you hinted to him with a grave melancholy face, that you were dying for his ſiſter—Gad-a-mercy, nephew! I will back thy modeſty againſt any other in the three kingdoms—It will do, Dick.

Belv. What could I do, uncle?—it was my laſt ſtake, and I play'd for a great deal.

Harc. You miſtake me, Dick——I don't ſay you could do better — I only can't account for your modeſty's doing ſo much; you have done ſuch wonders,
that

that I, who am rather bold than sheepish, have not yet ceas'd wondering at you. But do you think that you impos'd upon him?

Belv. Faith, I can't say——I am rather doubtful; he said very little, grumbled much, shook his head, and shew'd me the door.—But what success have you had with Alithea?

Harc. Just enough to have a glimmering of hope, without having light enough to see an inch before my nose.————This day will produce something; Alithea is a woman of great honour, and will sacrifice her happiness to it, unless Sparkish's absurdity stands my friend, and does every thing that the fates ought to do for me.

Belv. Yonder comes the prince of coxcombs, and if your mistress and mine should, by chance, be tripping this way, this fellow will spoil sport——let us avoid him—you can't cheat him before his face.

Harc. But I can tho', thanks to my wit, and his want of it; a foolish rival, and a jealous husband, assist their rivals designs, for they are sure to make their women hate them, which is their first step to their love for another man.

Belv. But you cannot come near his mistress but in his company.

Harc. Still the better for me, nephew, for fools are most easily cheated, when they themselves are accessaries; and he is to be bubbled of his mistress, or of his money (the common mistress) by keeping him company.

Enter Sparkish.

Spark. Who's that that is to be bubbled? faith, let me snack; I han't met with a bubble since Christmas. 'Gad, I think bubbles are like their brother-woodcocks, go out with the cold weather.

Harc. O pox! he did not hear all, I hope?

[*Apart to* Belville.

Spark. Come, you bubbling rogues, you, where do we sup? O Harcourt, my mistress tells me you have made love, fierce love to her last night, all the play long; ha, ha, ha! but I——

Harc. I make love to her !———

Spark. Nay, I forgive thee, and I know her, but I am sure I know myself.

Belv. Do you, fir? Then you are the wifeſt man in the world, and I honour you as ſuch.   [*Bowing.*

Spark. O your fervant, fir, you are at your raillery, are you?—You can't oblige me more—I'm your man —He'll meet with his match—Ha ! Harcourt !—Did not you hear me laugh prodigioufly at the play laſt night?

Harc. Yes, and was very much diſturb'd at it.— You put the actors and audience into confuſion—and all your friends out of countenance.

Spark. So much the better—I love confuſion—and to fee folks out of countenance—I was in tip-top fpirits, faith, and faid a thoufand good things.

Belv. But I thought you had gone to plays to laugh at the poet's good things, and not at your own?

Spark. Your fervant, fir : no, I thank you. 'Gad I go to a play, as to a country treat : I carry my own wine to one, and my own wit to t'other, or elſe I'm fure I fhould not be merry at either : and the reafon why we are fo often louder than the players, is, becauſe we hate authors damnably.

Belv. But why fhould you hate the poor rogues? you have too much wit, and defpife writing, I'm fure.

Spark. O yes, I defpife writing. But women, women, that make men do all foolifh things, make 'em write fongs too. Every body does it : 'tis e'en as common with lovers, as playing with fans ; and you can no more help rhyming to your Phillis, than drinking to your Phillis.

Harc. But the poets damn'd your fongs, did they?

Spark. O yes, damn the poets ; they turn'd them into burlefque, as they call it : that burlefque is a hocus pocus trick they have got, which, by the virtue of hictius doctius, topſy turvy, they make a clever witty thing abfolute nonfenfe ; do you know, Harcourt, that they ridicul'd my laſt fong, *twang twang*, the beſt I ever wrote?

Harc.

Harc. That may be, and be very eafily ridicul'd for all that.

Belv. Favour me with it, fir, I never heard it.

Spark. What, and have all the park about us ?

Harc. Which you'll not diflike, and fo, prithee, begin.

Spark. I never am afk'd twice, and fo have at you.

S O N G.

I.

Tell not me of the rofes and lillies,
Which tinge the fair cheek of your Phillis,
Tell not me of the dimples, and eyes,
For which filly Corydon dies ;
Let all whining lovers go hang,
　My heart would you hit,
　'Tip your arrow with wit,
And it comes to my heart with a twang, twang,
And it comes to my heart with a twang.

II.

I am rock to the handfome, and pretty,
Can only be touch'd by the witty ;
And beauty will ogle in vain,
　'The way to my heart's thro' my brain.
Let all whining lovers go hang,
　We wits, you muft know,
　Have two ftrings to our bow,
To return them their darts with a twang, twang,
And return them their darts with a twang.

At the end of the fong Harcourt *and* Belville *fteal away from* Sparkifh, *and leave him finging*——*He finks his voice by degrees, at the furprife of their being gone ; then*

　　　Enter Harcourt *and* Belville.

Spark. What the deuce did you go away for ?

Harc. Your miftrefs is coming.

Spark. The devil fhe is—O hide, hide me from her.　　　　　　　　[*Hides behind* Harcourt.

Harc. She fees you.

Spark. But I will not fee her: for I'm engag'd, and at this inftant. [*Looking at his watch.*

Harc. Pray firft take me, and reconcile me to her.

Spark. Another time : faith, it is to a lady, and one cannot make excufes to a woman.

Belv. You have need of 'em, I believe.

Spark. Pfhaw, prithee, hide me.

Moody, Peggy, *and* Alithea *appear.*

Harc. Your fervant, Mr. Moody.

Moody. Come along—— [*To* Peggy.

Peg. Lau !—what a fweet delightful place this is !

Moody. Come along, I fay——don't ftare about you fo——you'll betray yourfelf——
[*Exit* Moody *pulling* Peggy, Alithea *following.*

Harc. He does not know us——

Belv. Or he won't know us ——

Spark. So much the better——
[*Exit* Belville *after them at a diftance.*

Harc. Who is that pretty youth with him, Sparkifh ?

Spark. Some relation of Peggy's, I fuppofe, for he is fomething like her in face and gawkynefs.

Belville *returns.*

Belv. By all my hopes, uncle—Peggy in man's clothes—I am all over agitation. [*Afide to* Harc.

Harc. Be quiet, or you'll fpoil all. They return —— Alithea has feen you, Sparkifh, and will be angry if you don't go to her : befides, I would fain be reconcil'd to her, which none but you can do, my dear friend.

Spark. Well, that's a better reafon, dear friend : I would not go near her now for her's or my own fake ; but I can deny you nothing : for tho' I have known thee a great while, never go, if I do not love thee as well as a new acquaintance.

Harc. I am obliged to you, indeed, my dear friend : I wou'd be well with her, only to be well with thee ftill ; for thefe ties to wives ufually diffolve all ties to friends.

Spark. But they fhan't, tho'——Come along.
[*They retire.*
Re-enter

Re-enter Moody, *and* Peggy *in man's clothes,* Alithea *following.*

Moody. Sifter, if you will not go, we muft leave you—[*To* Alithea:]—The fool her gallant and fhe will mufter up all the young faunterers of this place. What a fwarm of cuckolds and cuckold-makers are here? I begin to be uneafy. [*Afide.*] Come, let's be gone, Peggy.

Peg. Don't you believe that, I han't half my belly-ful of fights yet.

Moody. Then walk this way.

Peg. Lord, what a power of fine folks are here. And Mr. Belville, as I hope to be married. [*Afide.*

Moody. Come along; what are you a muttering at?

Peg. There's the young gentleman there, you were fo angry about——that's in love with me.

Moody. No, no, he's a dangler after your fifter—or pretends to be—but they are all bad alike—Come along, I fay. [*He pulls her away.*

Peg. I'm glad to hear that—perhaps I may fit you, tho'. [*Exit with* Moody, Belville *eyeing them.*

Sparkifh, Harcourt, Alithea, *come forward.*

Spark. Come, dear madam, for my fake you fhall be reconcil'd to him.

Alith. For your fake I hate him.

Harc. That's fomething too cruel, madam, to hate me, for his fake.

Spark. Ay, indeed, madam, too, too cruel to me, to hate my friend for my fake.

Alith. I hate him, becaufe he is your enemy; and you ought to hate him too, for making love to me, if you love me.

Spark. That's a good one! I hate a man for loving you! If he did love you, 'tis but what he can't help; and 'tis your fault, not his, if he admires you.

Alith. Is it for your honour, or mine, to fuffer a man to make love to me, who am to marry you to-morrow?

Harc. But why, deareft madam, will you be more concerned for his honour than he is himfelf?

Let his honour alone for my fake and his. He has no honour.

Spark. How's that?

Harc. But what my dear friend can guard himfelf?

Spark. O ho ——— that's right again.

Alith. You aftonifh me, fir, with want of jealoufy.

Spark. And you make me giddy, madam, with your jealoufy and fears, and virtue and honour: 'Gad, I fee virtue makes a woman as troublefome as a little reading or learning.

Harc. Come, madam, you fee you ftrive in vain to make him jealous of me: my dear friend is the kindeft creature in the world to me.

Spark. Poor fellow!

Harc. But his kindnefs only is not enough for me, without your favour, your good opinion, dear madam: 'tis that muft perfect my happinefs. Good gentleman, he believes all I fay: wou'd you wou'd do fo. Jealous of me! I wou'd not wrong him nor you for the world.

Spark. Look you there: hear him, hear him, and not walk away fo. Come back again.

        [*Alithea walks carelefsly to and fro.*

Harc. I love you, madam, fo———

Spark. How's that! nay.—now you begin to go too far indeed.

Harc. So much, I confefs, I fay, I love you, that I would not have you miferable, and caft yourfelf away upon fo unworthy and inconfiderable a thing as what you fee here.

    [*Clapping his hand on his breaft, points to* Sparkifh.

Spark. No, faith, I believe thou wou'dft not; now his meaning is plain; but I knew before thou wou'df not wrong me, nor her.

Harc. No, no, Heav'ns forbid the glory of her fex fhou'd fall fo low, as, into the embraces of fuch a contemptible wretch, the leaft of mankind—my dear friend here—I injure him.

Alith. Very well.   [*Embracing* Sparkifh

Spark. No, no, dear friend, I knew it: madam,

you fee he will rather wrong himfelf than me in giving himfelf fuch names.

Alith. Do not you underftand him yet ?

Spark. Come, come, you fhall ftay till he has faluted you; that I may be affur'd you are friends, after his honeft advice and declaration : come, pray, madam, be friends with him.

Enter Moody *and* Peggy. Belville *at a diftance.*

Alith. You muft pardon me, fir, that I am not yet fo obedient to you.

Moody. What, invite your wife to kifs men ? Monftrous ! Are you not afham'd ? I will never forgive you. Let's be gone, fifter.

Spark. Are you not afham'd, that I fhou'd have more confidence in the chaftity of your family, than you have ?—You muft not teach me, I am a man of honour, fir, though I am frank and free; I am frank, fir——

Moody. Very frank, fir, to fhare your wife with your friends—You feem to be angry, and yet won't go. [*To* Alithea.

Alith. No impertinence fhall drive me away.

Moody. Becaufe you like it—But you ought to blufh at expofing your wife as you do.

Spark. What then ? It may be I have a pleafure in't, as I have to fhew fine clothes at a play-houfe, the firft day, and count money before poor rogues.

Moody. He that fhews his wife or money, will be in danger of having them borrowed fometimes.

Spark. I love to be envy'd, and would not marry a wife that I alone cou'd love. Loving alone is as dull as eating alone; and fo good-night, for I muft to Whitehall.—Madam, I hope you are now reconcil'd to my friend; and fo I wifh you a good-night, madam, and fleep if you can ; for to-morrow, you know, I muft vifit you early with a canonical gentleman. Good-night, dear Harcourt—remember to fend your brother. [*Exit* Sparkifh.

Harc. You may depend upon me. Madam, I hope you will not refufe my vifit to-morrow, if it fhould

fhould be earlier, with a canonical gentleman, than Mr. Sparkifh ?

Moody. This gentlewoman is yet under my care, therefore you muft yet forbear your freedom with her.   [*Coming between* Alithea *and* Harcourt.

Harc. Muft, fir !

Moody. Yes, fir, fhe is my fifter.

Harc. 'Tis well fhe is, fir——for I muft be her fervant, fir.——Madam——.

Moody. Come away, fifter, we had been gone if it had not been for you, and fo avoided thefe lewd rakehells, who feem to haunt us.

Harc. I fee a little time in the country makes a man turn wild and unfociable, and only fit to converfe with his horfes, dogs, and his herds.

Moody. I have bufinefs, fir, and muft mind it: your bufinefs is pleafure, therefore you and I muft go diff'rent ways.

Harc. Well, you may go on; but this pretty young gentleman [*takes hold of* Peggy] fhall ftay with us, for I fuppofe his bufinefs is the fame with ours, pleafure.

Moody. 'Sdeath, he knows her, fhe carries it fo fillily; yet if he does not, I fhou'd be more filly to difcover it firft.   [*Afide.*

' *Alith.* Pray, let him go, fir.'

Moody. Come, come.

Harc. Had you not rather ftay with us? [*To* Peggy.] Prithee, who is this pretty young fellow?

Moody. One to whom I am a guardian—I wifh I cou'd keep her out of your hands.   [*Afide.*

Harc. Who is he? I never faw any thing fo pretty in all my life.

Moody. Pfhaw, do not look upon him fo much, he's a poor bafhful youth, you'll put him out of countenance.   [*Offers to take her away.*

Harc. Here, nephew—let me introduce this young gentleman to your acquaintance—You are very like, and of the fame age, and fhould know one another—Salute him, Dick, à la Francoife.

[Belville *kiffes her.*
Moody.

Moody. I hate French fashions. Men kiss one another.   [*Endeavours to take hold of her.*

Peg. I am out of my wits——What do you kiss me
for ? I am no woman.

Harc. But you are ten times handsomer.

Peg. Nay, now you jeer one ; and pray don't jeer
me.

Harc. Kiss him again, Dick.

Moody. No, no, no ; come away, come away.
                    [*To* Peggy.

Harc. Why, what haste are you in ? Why won't
you let me talk with him ?

Moody. Because you'll debauch him, he's yet young
and innocent. How she gazes upon him ! The devil !
[*Aside.*] Come, pray let him go, I cannot stay fool-
ing any longer ; I tell you my wife stays supper for
us.

Harc. Does she ? Come then, we'll all go sup
with her.

Moody. No, no—now I think on't, having staid so
long for us, I warrant she's gone to bed—I wish she
and I were well out of your hands. [*Aside.*] Come, I
must rise early to-morrow ; come.————

Harc. Well then, if she be gone to-bed—I wish
her and you a good night. But pray, young gentleman, present my humble service to her.

Peg. Thank you heartily, sir.   [*Bowing.*

Moody. 'Sdeath, she will discover herself yet in
spite of me.   [*Aside.*

Belv. And mine too, sir.

Peg. That I will, indeed.   [*Bowing.*

Harc. Pray, give her this kiss for me.
                    [*Kisses* Peggy.

Moody. O heavens ! what do I suffer ?

Belv. And this for me.   [*Kisses* Peggy.

Peg. Thank you, sir.   [*Courtsies.*

Moody. O the idiot—now 'tis out—Ten thousand
cankers gnaw away their lips. Come, come, driv'ler.

' *Harc.* Good night, dear little gentleman. Ma-
' dam, good night—Farewell Moody—Come, ne-
' phew—have not I rais'd his jealous gall finely ?
                    ' [*Aside to* Belville.
                    ' *Belv.*

' *Belv.* A little too much, I fear.'

    [*Exeunt* Harcourt *and* Belville.

Moody. So, they are gone, at laſt. Siſter, ſtay with Peggy—'till I find my ſervant—don't let her ſtir an inch, I'll be back directly.   [*Exit* Moody.

   Harcourt *and* Belville *return.*

Harc. What, not gone yet ?—Nephew, ſhew the young gentleman Roſamond's pond, while I ſpeak another word to this lady.

Belv. Shall I have that pleaſure ?

Peg. With all my heart and ſoul, ſir.

    [*Exeunt* Belville *and* Peggy.

Alith. I cannot conſent to it indeed.

Harc. Let 'em look upon the place where ſo many deſpairing lovers have been deſtroy'd—You muſt indulge them—and me too in a few words.

    [Alithea *and* Harcourt *ſtruggle.*

Alith. My brother will go diſtracted—' tho' he de-
' ſerves to be vex'd a little for his brutality.'

Harc. My nephew is a very modeſt young man, you may depend upon his prudence.

Alith. Modeſt, prudent, and your nephew—I can't believe it, and I muſt follow them. ——   [*Going.*

    Enter Moody.

Moody. Where ! how !—what's become of—gone— whither ?———

' *Alith.* He's only gone with the young gentleman
' to ſee ſomething.

' *Moody.* Something ! ſee ſomething ! with a plague
' —where are they ?'

Alith. In the next walk only, brother.

Moody. Only, only, where, where ?   [*Exit.*

Harc. What's the matter with him ? Why ſo much concerned ? But, deareſt madam———

Alith. Pray let me go, ſir ; I have ſaid and ſuffered enough already.

Harc. Then you will not look upon, nor pity my ſufferings ?

Alith. To look upon 'em, when I cannot help 'em, were cruelty, not pity ; therefore I will never ſee you more.

       Enter

Enter Moody.

Moody. Gone, gone, not to be found ; quite gone ; ten thousand plagues go with 'em ; which way went they ?

Alith. But in t'other walk, brother.

Moody. T'other walk—t'other devil ! ' You are so ' full of vanity, and fond of admiration, that you'll ' suffer your own honour and mine to run any risque ' rather than not indulge your inordinate desire of ' flattery'—Where are they, I say ?

Alith. You are too abusive, brother, and too violent about trifles ; therefore let your jealousy search for them, for I know nothing of 'em.

Moody. You know where they are, you infamous wretch, eternal shame of your family ; which you do not dishonour enough yourself, you think, but you must help her to it too, thou legion of———

Alith. Good brother———

Moody. False, false sister———   [*Exit.*

Alith. Shew me to my chair, Mr. Harcourt—His scurrility has overpower'd me—I will get rid of his tyranny and your importunities, and give my hand to Sparkish to-morrow morning.   [*Exeunt.*

SCENE *changes to another part of the Park.*

Enter Belville *and* Miss Peggy.

Belv. No disguise could conceal you from my heart ; I pretended not to know you, that I might deceive the dragon that continually watches over you—but now he's asleep, let us fly from misery to happiness.

Peg. Indeed, Mr. Belville, as well as I like you, I can't think of going away with you so—and as much as I hate my guardian, I must take leave of him a little handsomely, or he will kill me, so he will.

Belv. But, dear Miss Peggy, think of your situation ; if we don't make the best use of this opportunity, we never may have another.

Peg. Ay, but Mr. Belville—I am as good as married already—my guardian has contracted me, and
there

there wants nothing but church ceremony to make us one—I call him husband, and he calls me wife already : he made me do so ;—and we had been married in church long ago, if the writings could have been finish'd.

Belv. That's his deceit, my sweet creature—He pretends to have married you, for fear of your liking any body else—You have a right to chuse for yourself, and there is no law in heaven or earth, that binds you before marriage to a man you cannot like.

Peg. I'fack, no more I believe it does ; sister Alithea's maid has told me as much—she's a very sensible girl.

Belv. You are in the very jaws of perdition, and nothing but running away can avoid it——the law will finish your chains to-morrow, and the church will rivet them the day after——Let us secure our happiness by escape, and Love and Fortune will do the rest for us.

Peg. These are fine sayings, to be sure, Mr. Belville ; but how shall we get my fortune out of Bud's clutches ? We must be a little cunning ; 'tis worth trying for——We can at any time run away without it.

Belv. I see by your fears, my dear Peggy, that you live in awe of this brutal guardian ; and if he has you once more in his possession, both you and your fortune are secured to him for ever.

Peg. Ay, but it shan't tho'—I thank him for that.

Belv. If you marry without his consent, he can but seize upon half your fortune—The other half, and a younger brother's fortune, with a treasure of love, are our own— Take it, my sweetest Peggy, and this moment, or we shall be divided for ever.

[*Kneels and presses her hand.*

Peg. I'fackins, but we won't—Your fine talk has bewitch'd me.

Belv. 'Tis you have bewitch'd me—thou dear, inchanting, sweet simplicity——Let us fly with the wings of love to my house there, and we shall be safe for ever.

Peg.

Peg. And fo we will then—there fqueeze me again by the hand; now run away with me, and if my guardy follows us, the devil take the hindmoft, I fay. [*Going.*] Boo! here he is.

Enter Moody *haftily, and meets them.*

Belv. Curft fortune!

Moody. O! there's my ftray'd fheep, and the wolf again in fheep's cloathing!—Now I have recover'd her, I fhall come to my fenfes again—Where have you been, you puppy?

Peg. Been, Bud?—We have been hunting all over the park to find you.

Belv. From one end to the other, fir. [*Confufedly.*

Moody. But not where I was to be found, you young devil you—Why did you ftart when you faw me?

Peg. I'm always frighten'd when I fee you, and if I did not love you fo well—I fhould run away from you, fo I fhould.   [*Pouting.*

Moody. But I'll take care you don't.

Peg. This gentleman has a favour to beg of you, Bud.   [Belville *makes figns of diflike.*

Moody. I am not in the humour to grant favours to young gentlemen, tho' you may—What have you been doing with this young lady?—gentleman, I would fay—Bliffers on my tongue!

Peg. Fie, Bud, you have told all.

Belv. I have been as civil as I could to the young ftranger; and if you'll permit me, I will take the trouble off your hands, and fhew the young fpark Rofamond's Pond, for he has not feen it yet——Come, pretty youth, will you go with me?   [*Goes to her.*

Peg. As my guardian pleafes.

Moody. No, no, it does not pleafe me—whatever I think he ought to fee, I fhall fhow him myfelf—You may vifit Rofamond's Pond, if you will—and the bottom of it, if you will—And fo, fir, your humble fervant.   [*Exit with* Mifs *under his arm.*

Belv. What curfed luck! [*ftamps.*] to be prevented at the very inftant of my carrying off the golden fleece!——We have now rais'd his fufpicions to fuch

a degree,

a degree, that he'll lock her up directly—sign articles this night—marry her in the morning—and away
from the church into the country.——What a miferable fituation am I in!—I have love enough to be a
knight-errant in the caufe—I will lofe my life, or
refcue my Dulcinea—I have hopes in her fpirit too—
for at the worft fhe can open her window, throw herfelf into my arms, from thence into a poft-chaife, and
away for the Tweed as faft as love and four poft-hor-
fes can carry us.   [*Exit.*

ACT IV. SCENE, Moody's *Houfe.*

Lucy, Alithea *dreffed.*

Lucy. WELL, madam, now I have drefs'd you,
and fet you out with fo many ornaments,
and fpent fo much time upon you, and all this for no
other purpofe but to bury you alive ; for I look upon
Mr. Sparkifh's bed to be little better than a grave.

Alith. Hold your peace.

Lucy. Nay, madam, I will afk you the reafon
why you wou'd banifh poor Mr. Harcourt for ever
from your fight ? how cou'd you be fo hard-hearted ?

Alith. 'Twas becaufe I was not hard-hearted.

Lucy. No, no ; 'twas ftark love and kindnefs, I
warrant ?

Alith. It was fo ; I wou'd fee him no more, becaufe
I love him.

Lucy. Hey-day ! a very pretty reafon.

Alith. You do not underftand me.

Lucy. I wifh you may yourfelf.

Alith. I was engag'd to marry, you fee, another
man, whom my juftice will not fuffer me to deceive
or injure.

Lucy. Can there be a greater cheat or wrong done
to a man, than to give him your perfon, without
your heart ? I fhou'd make a confcience of it.

Alith. I'll retrieve it for him after I am married.

Lucy.

Lucy. The woman that marries to love better, will be as much miftaken, as the rake that marries to live better.

Alith. What nonfenfe you talk!

Lucy. 'Tis a melancholy truth, madam—Marrying to increafe love, is like gaming to become rich——Alas! you only lofe what little ftock you had before ——There are many woeful examples of it in this righteous town!

Alith. I find by your rhetoric you have been brib'd to betray me.

Lucy. Only by his merit, that has brib'd your heart, you fee, againft your word and rigid honour.

Alith. Come, pray talk no more of honour, nor Mr. Harcourt; I wifh the other would come to fecure my fidelity to him, and his right in me.

Lucy. You will marry him then?

Alith. Certainly; I have given him already my word, and will my hand too, to make it good when he comes.

Lucy. Well, I wifh I may never ftick a pin more, if he be not an errant natural to t'other fine gentleman.

Alith. I own he wants the wit of Harcourt, which I will difpenfe withal for another want he has, which is want of jealoufy, which men of wit feldom want.

Lucy. Lord, madam, what fhou'd you do with a fool to your hufband? You intend to be honeft, don't you? Then that hufbandly virtue, credulity, is thrown away upon you.

Alith. He only that cou'd fufpect my virtue, fhou'd have caufe to do it? 'tis Sparkifh's confidence in my truth, that obliges me to be faithful to him.

Lucy. What, faithful to a creature who is incapable of loving and efteeming you as he ought!—To throw away your beauty, wit, accomplifhments, fweet-temper——

Alith. Hold your tongue.

Lucy. That you know I can't do, madam; and upon this occafion, I will talk for ever—What, give yourfelf away to one, that poor I, your maid, would not accept of?

Alith.

Alith. How, Lucy!

Lucy. I would not, upon my honour, madam; 'tis never too late to repent—Take a man, and give up your coxcomb, I fay.

Enter Servant.

Serv. Mr. Sparkifh, with company, madam, attends you below.

Alith. I will wait upon 'em. [*Exit Servant.*] My heart begins to fail me, but I muft go through with it. Go with me, Lucy. [*Exit.*

Lucy. Not I, indeed, madam——If you will leap the precipice, you fhall fall by yourfelf—What excellent advice have I thrown away!—So I'll e'en take it where it will be more welcome.——Mifs Peggy is bent upon mifchief againft her guardian, and fhe can't have a better privy-counfellor than myfelf—I muft be bufy one way or another. [*Exit.*

SCENE, *a Chamber in* Moody's *Houfe.*

Moody *and* Mifs Peggy.

Moody. I faw him kifs your hand before you faw me. This pretence of liking my fifter was all a blind—the young abandon'd hypocrite! [*afide.*] Tell me, I fay, for I know he likes you, and was hurrying you to his houfe—tell me, I fay——

Peg. Lord, han't I told it a hundred times over?

Moody. I would try if, in the repetition of the ungrateful tale, I cou'd find her altering it in the leaft circumftance, for if her ftory be falfe, fhe is fo too. [*Afide.*] Come, how was't, baggage?

Peg. Lord, what pleafure you take to hear it, fure?

Moody. No, you take more in telling it, I find; but fpeak, how was't? no lyes—I faw him kifs you— he kifs'd you before my face.

Peg. Nay, you need not be fo angry with him neither; for, to fay truth, he has the fweeteft breath I ever knew.

Moody. The devil!—you were fatisfy'd with it then, and would do it again?——

Peg. Not unlefs he fhou'd force me.

Moody.

Moody. Force you, changeling.

Peg. If I had ftruggled too much, you know—he wou'd have known I had been a woman; fo I was quiet, for fear of being found out.

Moody. If you had been in petticoats, you wou'd have knock'd him down, wou'd not you?

Peg. With what, Bud?—I cou'd not help myfelf —befides, he did it fo modeftly, and blufh'd fo—that I almoft thought him a girl in men's cloaths, and upon his mummery too as well as me—and if fo, there was no harm done, you know.

Moody. This is worfe and worfe—fo 'tis plain fhe loves him, yet fhe has not love enough to make her conceal it from me; but the fight of him will encreafe her averfion for me, and love for him; and that love inftruct her how to deceive me, and fatisfy him, all idiot as fhe is: Love, 'twas he gave women firft their craft, their art of deluding; ' out of Nature's ' hands they came plain, open, filly, and fit for flaves, ' as fhe and Heaven intended 'em, but damn'd Love ' —well'—I muft ftrangle that little monfter, whilft I can deal with him. [*Afide.*]—Go, fetch pen, ink, and paper out of the next room.

Peg. Yes, I will, Bud. What's the matter now? [*Afide.*] [*Exit.*

Moody. This young fellow loves her, and fhe loves him—the reft is all hypocrify—How the young modeft villain endeavour'd to deceive me! But I'll crufh this mifchief in the fhell—Why fhould women have more invention in love than men? It can only be, becaufe they have more defire; more foliciting paffions, more of the devil. |*Afide.*] [*Enter* Mifs Peggy.] Come, minx, fit down and write.

Peg. Ay, dear, dear Bud; but I can't do't very well.

Moody. I wifh you could not at all.

Peg. But what fhould I write for?

Moody. I'll have you write a letter to this young man.

Peg. O Lord, to the young gentleman a letter.

Moody. Yes, to the young gentleman.

Peg.

Peg. Lord, you do but jeer : fure you jeſt.

Moody. I am not ſo merry : come, fit down, and write as I bid you.

Peg. What do you think I am a fool ?

Moody. She's afraid I wou'd not dictate any love to him, therefore ſhe's unwilling [*Aſide.*]—But you had beſt begin.

Peg. Indeed and indeed but I won't, ſo I won't.

Moody. Why ?

Peg. Becauſe he's in town; you may ſend for him here, if you will.

Moody. Very well, you wou'd have him brought to you ?—is it come to this ? I ſay, take the pen and ink and write, or you'll provoke me.

Peg. Lord, what d'ye make a fool of me for ? Don't I know that letters are never writ but from the country to London, and from London into the country ! now he's in town, and I am in town too ; therefore I can't write to him, you know.

Moody. So, I am glad it is no worſe ; ſhe is innocent enough yet. [*Aſide.*] Yes, you may, when your huſband bids, write letters to people that are in town.

Peg. O may I ſo ! then I am ſatisfied.

Moody. Come, begin—*Sir*— [*Dictates.*

Peg. Shan't I ſay, *Dear Sir?* you know one ſays always ſomething more than bare Sir.

Moody. Write as I bid you, or I will write ſomething with this pen-knife in your face.

Peg. Nay, good Bud—*Sir*— [*writes.*

Moody. *Though I ſuffer'd laſt night your nauſeous loath'd kiſſes and embraces*—Write !

Peg. Nay, why ſhould I ſay ſo ? you know I told you he had a ſweet breath.

Moody. Write !

Peg. Let me put out *loath'd* ?

Moody. Write, I ſay.

Peg. Well then. [*writes.*

Moody. Let me ſee what you have writ. *Tho' I ſuffer'd laſt night your kiſſes and embraces*—[*reads the paper.*] Thou impudent creature, where is *nauſeous* and *loath'd* ?

Peg.

Peg. I can't abide to write fuch filthy words.

Moody. Once more write as I'd have you, and queftion it not, or I will fpoil your writing with this ; I will ftab out thofe eyes that caufe my mifchief.

[*Holds up the penknife.*

Peg. O Lord, I will.

Moody. So—fo—let's fee now ! *tho' I fuffered laft night your naufeous loath'd kiffes and embraces ; go on —yet I would not have you prefume that you fhall ever repeat them——fo.* [*She writes.*

Peg. I have writ it.

Moody. O then—*I- then conceal'd myfelf from your knowledge, to avoid your infolencies*—— [*She writes.*

Peg. To avoid——

Moody. .*Your infolencies*————

Peg. Your infolencies. [*Writes !*

Moody. The fame reafon, now I am out of your hands—

Peg. So——· [*She writes.*

Moody. Makes me own to you my unfortunate—tho' in-nocent frolick of being in man's clothes. [*She writes.*

Peg. So——·

Moody. That you may for evermore——

Peg. Evermore ?

Moody. Evermore ceafe to purfue her, who hates and detefts you. [*She writes.*

Peg. So—h. [*Sighs.*

Moody. .What do you figh for ?—*detefts you—as much as fhe loves her hufband and her honour*—

Peg. I vow, hufband, he'll ne'er believe I fhou'd write fuch a letter.

Moody. What, he'd expect a kinder from you ? Come, now your name only.

Peg. What, fhan't I fay your moft faithful humble fervant till death ?

Moody. No, tormenting fiend——Her ftile, I find, wou'd be very foft. [*Afide.*] Come, wrap it up now, whilft I go fetch wax and a candle, and write on the outfide, *For Mr. Belville.* [*Exit* Moody.

Peg. For Mr. *Belville*—fo—I am glad he is gone— Hark ! I hear a noife ! [*goes to the door.*] ifeck there's folks with him—that's pure——now I may think a

C little

little——Why should I send dear Mr. Belville such a letter?—Can one have no shift? ah! a London woman wou'd have had a hundred presently.—— Stay——what if I should write a letter, and wrap it up like this, and write upon't too?——Ay, but then my guardian wou'd see't——I don't know what to do——But yet y'vads I'll try, so I will—for I will not send this letter to poor Mr. Belville, come what will on't. [*She writes, and repeats what she writes.*] *Dear, sweet, Mr. Belville—so—My guardian wou'd have me send you a base, rude letter, but I won't—so— and wou'd have me say, I hate you—but I won't—— there——for I'm sure if you and I were in the country at cards together—so—I cou'd not help treading on your toe under the table——so pray keep at home, for I shall be with you as soon as I can——so no more at present from one who am, dear, dear, poor, dear Mr. Belville, your loving friend till death, Margaret Thrift.——* So—now wrap it up just like t'other—so—now write, *For Mr. Belville*—But oh! what shall I do with it? for here comes my guardian.

Enter Moody.

Moody. I have been detained by a sparkish coxcomb, who pretended a visit to me, but I fear 'twas to my wife. [*Aside.*] What, have you done?

Peg. Ay, ay, Bud, just now.

Moody. Let's see't; what d'ye tremble for?——
[*He opens and reads the first letter.*

Peg. So I had been serv'd if I had given him this.
[*Aside.*

Moody. Come, where's the wax and seal?

Peg. Lord, what shall I do now? Nay, then I have it—[*Aside.*]—pray let me see't. Lord, you think me so errand a fool, I cannot seal a letter; I will do't, so I will. [*Snatches the letter from him, changes it for the other, seals it, and delivers it to him.*]

Moody. Nay, I believe you will learn that and other things too, which I wou'd not have you.

Peg. So, han't I done it curiously? I think I have —there's my letter going to Mr. Belville, since he'll needs have me send letters to folks. [*Aside.*
Moody.

Moody. 'Tis very well, but I warrant you wou'd not have it go now?

Peg. Yes, indeed, but I wou'd, Bud, now.

Moody. Well, you are a good girl then. Come, let me lock you up in your chamber, till I come back ; and be fure you come not within three ftrides of the window, when I am gone ; for I have a fpy in the ftreet. [*Puts her into the chamber.*] At leaft 'tis fit fhe thinks fo ; if we do not cheat women, they'll cheat us, and fraud may be juftly ufed with fecret enemies, of which a wife is the moft dangerous ; and he that has a handfome one to keep, and a frontier town, muft provide againft treachery rather than open force ——Now I have fecured all within, I'll deal with the foe without, with falfe intelligence. ' This will ' dafh all his impudent hopes [*holds up the letter*] at ' once, and I fhall fleep now fecurely in my garrifon, ' without fear of furprize—But no time is to be loft ' —I'll fteal a march upon him.' [*Exit.*

SCENE *changes to* Belville's *lodgings.*

Enter Lucy *and* Belville.

Lucy. I run great rifques, to be fure, to ferve the young lady, and you, fir——but I know you are a gentleman of honour, and wou'd fcorn to betray a friend who means you well, and is above being mercenary.

Belv. As you are not mercenary, Mrs. Lucy, I ought to be the more generous—give me leave to prefent you with this trifle, [*gives a ring.*] not as a reward for fervices, but as a fmall token of friendfhip.

Lucy. Tho' I fcorn to be brib'd in any caufe, yet I am proud to accept it, as a mark of your regard, and as fuch fhall keep it for your fake—and now to bufinefs.

Belv. You flatter me then, that Mifs Peggy has the moft rooted averfion for her guardian, and fome prejudices in my favour.

Lucy.

Lucy. She has intrufted me with her very thoughts and I have rais'd her difobedience to fuch a pitch, that fhe would have opened her whole heart to you in a letter, had we not been interrupted by her brutal guardian.

Belv. She told me in the Park, that you had con- vinced her fhe was not married to him.

Lucy. There was not much difficulty in that; but if any thing could have frighten'd her into that be- lief, her filthy guardian had done it—He made her almoft believe, that the faving her foul depended up- on marrying him—Did you ever hear of fuch a repro- bate ?

Belv. How I adore her bewitching fimplicity !

Lucy. Simplicity, fir ! fhe's able to make a fool of any of us—If I had half her wit, I would not conti- nue long in fervice, as well as I love my miftrefs.

Belv. But, dear Lucy, what can Mifs Peggy pro- pofe ?

Lucy. To run away from her guardian, and marry you.

Belv. She might have done both, and loft the op- portunity.

Lucy. She will do both, and make an opportunity, if it does not come of itfelf. The thoughts of run- ning away, or of being married, when taken fepa- rately, will put any maiden of us into great confu- fion ; but when they come both together, are too much for the boldeft of us——Mifs Peggy was over- power'd with your propofal, and no wonder fhe could not determine for the beft ; I fhould have been a little frighten'd myfelf.

Belv. But has the dear creature refolv'd ?

Lucy. Has fhe—why, fhe will run away and marry you, in fpite of your teeth, the firft moment fhe can break prifon—fo you, in your turn, muft take care not to have your qualms——I have known feveral bold gentlemen not able to draw their fwords, when a challenge has come too quick upon 'em.

Belv. I affure you, Mrs. Lucy, that I am no bully in love, and mifs Peggy will meet with her match, come when fhe will.

Lucy.

Lucy. Ay, fo you all fay, but talking does no bufinefs—Stay at home till you hear from us.

Belv. Bleffings on thee, Lucy, for the thought.

Moody, *fpeaking without.*

Moody. But I muft and will fee him, let him have
what company he will.

Lucy. As I hope to be marry'd, Mr. Belville, I
hear Mr. Moody's voice—Where fhall I hide myfelf?
—if he fees me, we are all undone.

Belv. This is our curfed luck again—What the
devil can he want here?—I have loft my fenfes—get
into this clofet till he's gone. [*Puts* Lucy *into the clofet.*] This vifit means fomething; I am quite con-
founded—Don't you ftir, Lucy—I muft put the beft
face upon the matter———— Now for it————
[*Takes a book and reads.*

Enter Moody.

Moody. You will excufe me, fir, for breaking thro'
forms, and your fervant's entreaties, to have the honour—but you are alone, fir—your fellow told me
below that you were with company.

Belv. Yes, fir, the beft company. [*Shews his book.*]
When I converfe with my betters, I choofe to have
'em alone.

Moody. And I chofe to interrupt your converfation; the bufinefs of my errand muft plead my excufe.

Belv. You fhall be always welcome to me—but
you feem ruffled, fir; what brings you hither, and fo
feemingly out of humour?

Moody. Your impertinency—I beg pardon—your
modefty, I mean.

Belv. My impertinency!

Moody. Your impertinency.

Belv. Sir, from the peculiarity of your character,
and your intimacy with my uncle, I fhall allow you
great privileges; but you muft confider, youth has its
privileges too; and as I have not the honour of your
acquaintance, I am not oblig'd to bear with your ill-
humours or your ill-manners.

Moody. They who wrong me, young man, muft

C 3   bear

bear with both ; and if you had not made too free
with me, I fhould have taken no liberties with you.

' *Belv.* I don't underftand you, fir ; but you gen-
' tlemen, who have handfome wives, think you have
' a privilege of faying any thing to us young fellows,
' and are as brutifh as if you were our creditors.

' *Moody.* I fhan't truft you any way.

' *Belv.* But why fo diffident, fir ? you don't know
' me.

' *Moody.* I am not diffident, young man, but cer-
' tain, becaufe I think I do know you.'

Belv. I could have wifh'd, fir, to have found you a
little more civil, the firft time I have the honour of a
vifit from you.

Moody. If that is all you want, young gentleman,
you will find me very civil indeed ! There, fir, read
that, and let your modefty declare whether I want
either kindnefs or civility—Look you there, fir.

[Gives a letter.

Belv. What is't ?

Moody. Only a love-letter, fir ;——and from my
wife.

Belv. How, is it from your wife ?—hum and hum.

[Reads.

Moody. Even from my wife, fir ; am not I wond'rous
kind and civil to you now too ? But you'll not think
her fo. [Afide.

Belv. Ha, is this a trick of his or her's ? [Afide.

Moody. The gentleman's furpriz'd, I find ? what,
you expected a kinder letter?

Belv. No, faith, not I ; how cou'd I ?

Moody. Yes, yes, I'm fure you did ; a man fo
young, and well made as you are, muft needs be dif-
appointed, if the women declare not their paffion at
the firft fight or opportunity.

Belv. But what fhou'd this mean ? It feems he
knows not what the letter contains ! [Afide.

Moody. Come, ne'er wonder at it fo much.

Belv. Faith, I can't help it.

Moody. Now, I think, I have deferv'd your infinite
friendfhip

friendſhip and kindneſs, and have ſhew'd myſelf ſuf-
ficiently an obliging kind friend and huſband—am I
not ſo, to bring a letter from my wife to her gallant ?

Belv. Ay, indeed, you are the moſt obliging kind
friend and huſband in the world ; ha, ha, ha ! Pray,
however, preſent my humble ſervice to her, and tell
her, I will obey her letter to a tittle, and fulfil her
deſires, be what they will, or with what difficulty
ſoever I do't ; and you ſhall be no more jealous of
me, I warrant her, and you.

Moody. Well then, fare you well, and play with
any man's honour but mine, kiſs any man's wife but
mine, and welcome—ſo, Mr. Modeſty, your ſervant.

-[*As* Moody *is going out he is met by* Sparkiſh.

Spark. So, brother-in-law, that was to have been,
I have follow'd you from home to Belville's : I have
ſtrange news for you.

Moody. What, are you wiſer than you were this
morning ?

Spark. Faith I don't know but I am, for I have
loſt your ſiſter, and I ſhan't eat half an ounce the leſs
at dinner for it ; there's philoſophy for you.

Moody Inſenſibility, you mean—I hope you don't
mean to uſe my ſiſter ill, ſir ?

Spark. No, ſir, ſhe has uſed me ill ; ſhe's in her
tantrums—I have had a narrow eſcape, ſir.

Moody. If thou art endow'd with the ſmalleſt por-
tion of underſtanding, explain this riddle.

Belv. Ay, ay, prithee, Sparkiſh—condeſcend to
be intelligible.

Spark. Why, you muſt know—we had ſettled to
be married—it is the ſame thing to me, whether I am
married or not—I have no particular fancy one way or
another, and ſo I told your ſiſter ; off or on, 'tis the
ſame thing to me ; but the thing was fix'd, you,
know—You and my aunt brought it about—I had no
hand in it. And, to ſhew you that I was as willing
to marry your ſiſter as any other woman, I ſuffered
the law to tye me up to hard terms, and the church
would have finiſh'd me ſtill to harder—but ſhe was
taken with her tantrums !

Moody.

Moody. Damn your tantrums—come to the point.

Spark. Your fifter took an averfion to the parfon, Frank Harcourt's brother—abus'd him like a pickpocket, and fwore 'twas Harcourt himfelf.

Moody. And fo it was, for I faw him.

Spark. Here's fine work!—why, you are as mad as your fifter—I tell you it was Ned, Frank's twin brother.

Moody. What, Frank told you fo?

Spark. Ay, and Ned too——they were both in a ftory.

Moody. What an incorrigible fellow!——Come, come, I muft be gone.

Spark. Nay, nay, you fhall hear my ftory out.—— She walk'd up within piftol-fhot of the church—then twirl'd round upon her heel—call'd me every name fhe could think of; and when fhe had exhaufted her imagination, and tir'd her tongue—no eafy matter, let me tell you—fhe call'd her chair, fent her footman to buy a monkey before my face, then bid me good-morrow with a fneer, and left us with our mouths open in the middle of a hundred people, who were all laughing at us! If thefe are not tantrums, I don't know what are.

Moody. Ha, ha, ha! I thank thee, Sparkifh, from my foul; 'tis a moft exquifite ftory; I have not had fuch a laugh for this half year—Thou art a moft ridiculous puppy, and I am infinitely oblig'd to thee; ha, ha, ha! [*Exit* Moody.

Spark. Did you ever hear the like, Belville?

Belv. O yes; how is it poffible to hear fuch a foolifh ftory, and fee thy foolifh face, and not laugh at 'em; ha, ha, ha!

Lucy *in the clofet laughs.*

Spark. Hey-day! what's that? What, have you rais'd a devil in the clofet, to make up a laughing chorus at me? I muft take a peep————

[*Going to the clofet.*

Belv. Indeed but you muft not.

Spark. 'Twas a woman's voice.

Belv. So much the better for me.

Spark.

Spark. Prithee, introduce me.

Belv. Though you take a pleasure in expofing your ladies, I choofe to conceal mine. So, my dear Sparkifh, left the lady fhould be fick by too long a confinement, and laughing heartily at you—I muft entreat you to withdraw—Prithee, excufe me, I muft laugh—ha, ha, ha, ha!

Spark. Do you know that I begin to be angry, Belville?

Belv. I can't help that; ha, ha, ha!

Spark. My character's at ftake—I fhall be thought a damn'd filly fellow—I will call Alithea to an account directly. [*Exit.*

Belv. Ha, ha, ha!

Lucy *peeping out.*

Lucy. Ha, ha, ha! O dear fir, let me have my laugh out, or I fhall burft—What an adventure! [*Laughs.*

Belv. My fweet Peggy has fent me the kindeft letter—and by the dragon himfelf—There's a fpirit for you!

Lucy. There's fimplicity for you! Shew me a town-bred girl with half the genius—Send you a love-letter, and by a jealous guardian too! ha, ha, ha! 'Tis too much—too much ———

Belv. She begs me to ftay at home—for fhe intends to run away with me, the firft opportunity.

Lucy. And, to complete the whole, my miftrefs is deliver'd from her fool too—Ha, ha, ha! I fhall die; ha, ha, ha!—' Dear Mr. Belville, laugh, laugh, I ' befeech you laugh.

' *Belv.* I do, I do, my dear Lucy, and I hope we ' never fhall have caufe to be lefs merry as long as we ' live—ha, ha, ha!'

Lucy. ' O never, never—I fhall certainly die'— Well, Mr. Belville—the world goes as it fhould do— my miftrefs will exchange her fool for a wit, Mifs Peggy her brute for a pretty young fellow; I fhall dance at two weddings—be well rewarded by both parties—get a huſband myſelf, and be as happy as the beſt of you—and ſo your humble ſervant. [*Exit.*

Belv. Succeſs attend you, Lucy——— [*Exit.*

ACT V. SCENE, Moody's *houſe.*

Miſs Peggy *alone, leaning on her elbow. A table, pen, ink, and paper.*

Peg. WELL, 'tis e'en ſo, I have got the London diſeaſe they call love ; I am ſick of my guardian, and dying for Mr. Belville! I have heard this diſtemper call'd a fever, but methinks it is liker an ague ; for, when I think of my guardian, I tremble, and am in a cold ſweat ; but when I think of my gallant, dear Mr. Belville, my hot fit comes, and I am all in a fever indeed : my own chamber is tedious to me, and I would fain be remov'd to his, and then methinks I ſhou'd be very well. Ah! poor Mr. Belville! Well, I cannot, will not ſtay here ; therefore I'll make an end of my letter to him, which ſhall be a finer letter than my laſt, becauſe I have ſtudied it like any thing. Oh! ſick, ſick!

Enter Moody, *who, ſeeing her writing, ſteals ſoftly behind her, and looking over her ſhoulder, ſnatches the paper from her.*

Moody. What, writing more letters?

Peg. O Lord! Bud, why d'ye fright me ſo?

[*She offers to run out, he ſtops her and reads.*

Moody. How's this! nay, you ſhall not ſtir, madam. *Dear, dear, dear Mr. Belville,*—very well, I have taught you to write letters to good purpoſe—but let's ſee't.—[*Reads.*]—*Firſt, I am to beg your pardon for my boldneſs in writing to you, which I'd have you to know I would not have done, had you not ſaid firſt you lov'd me ſo extremely ; which, if you do, you will never ſuffer me to be another man's, who I loath, nauſeate, and deteſt :* (now you can write theſe filthy words.) But what follows?—*therefore, I hope you will*

will speedily find some way to free me from this unfortu-
nate match, which was never, I assure you, of my
choice, but I'm afraid 'tis already too far gone ; how-
ever, if you love me, as I do you, you will try what you
can do ; you must help me away before to-morrow, or
else, alas! I shall be for ever out of your reach, for I
can defer no longer our—our—(what is to follow our—
speak what) our journey into the country, I suppose.
—Oh, woman, damn'd woman! and love, damn'd .
love! their old tempter ; for this is one of his mira-
cles : in a moment he can make those blind that
cou'd see, and those see that were blind ; those dumb
that cou'd speak, and those prattle who were dumb
before ; nay, what is more than all, make those
dough-bak'd, senseless, indocile animals, women,
too hard for us, their politic lords and rulers, in a
moment. But make an end of your letter, and then
I'll make an end of you thus, and all my plagues together.   [*Draws his sword.*

Peg. O Lord! O Lord! you are such a passionate
man, Bud!

Moody. Come, take the pen, and make an end of
the letter, just as you intended ; if you are false in a
tittle, I shall soon perceive it, and punish you with
this, as you deserve. [*Lays his hand on his sword.*]
Write what was to follow—let's see——(*You must
make haste and help me away before to-morrow, or else
I shall be for ever out of your reach, for I can defer no
longer our)* what follows our ?————

                    [Peggy *takes the pen and writes.*

Peg. Must all out then, Bud ?——Look you there
then.

Moody. Let's see——(*for I can defer no longer our
wedding*———*Your slighted* Alithea.) What's the
meaning of this, my sister's name to't ? speak, un-
riddle.

Peg. Yes, indeed, Bud.

Moody. But why her name to't ? speak——speak,
I say.

Peg. Ay, but you'll tell her again : if you wou'd
not tell her again——

Moody. I will not; I am ftunn'd, my head turns round. Speak.

Peg. Won't you tell her indeed, and indeed?

Moody. No; fpeak, I fay.

Peg. She'll be angry with me; but I had rather fhe fhould be angry with me than you, Bud. And to tell you the truth, 'twas fhe made me write the letter, and taught me what I fhould write.

Moody. Ha!—I thought the ftyle was fomewhat better than her own. [*Afide.*] Cou'd fhe come to you to teach you, fince I had lock'd you up alone?

Peg. Oh, thro' the key-hole, Bud.

Moody. But why fhou'd fhe make you write a letter for her to him, fince fhe can write herfelf?

Peg. Why, fhe faid becaufe——for I was unwilling to do it.

Moody. Becaufe, what——becaufe————

Peg. Becaufe, left Mr. Belville, as he was fo young, fhou'd be inconftant, and refufe her, or be vain afterwards, and fhew the letter, fhe might difown it, the hand not being hers.

Moody. Belville again!——Am I to be deceiv'd again with that young hypocrite?

Peg. You have deceiv'd yourfelf; Bud, you have indeed——I have kept the fecret for my fifter's fake, as long as I could——but you muft know it——and fhall know it too. [*Cries.*

Moody. Dry your eyes.

Peg. You always thought he was hankering after me—Good law! he's dying for Alithea, and Alithea for him—they have had private meetings—and he was making love to her before yefterday, from the tavern-window, when you thought it was to me——I would have difcover'd all—but fhe made me fwear to deceive you, and fo I have finely—have not I, Bud?

Moody. Why did you write that foolifh letter to him then, and make me more foolifh to carry it?

Peg. To carry on the joke, Bud—to oblige them?

Moody. And will nothing ferve her but that taper jackanapes, that great baby?—he's too young for her to marry.

Peg.

Peg. Why do you marry me then ? 'tis the fame thing, Bud.

Moody. No, no, 'tis quite different—How innocent fhe is !—This changeling cou'd not invent this lye ; but if fhe cou'd, why fhou'd fhe ? She might think I fhould foon difcover it. [*Afide.*]—But hark you, madam, your fifter went out in the morning, and I have not feen her within fince.

Peg. Alack-a-day, fhe has been crying all day above, it feems, in a corner.

Moody. Where is fhe ? let me fpeak with her.

Peg. O Lord ! then fhe'll difcover all.—[*Afide.*] Pray hold, Bud ; what, d'ye mean to difcover me ! fhe'll know I have told you then. Pray, Bud, let me talk with her firft.

Moody. I muft fpeak with her, to know whether Belville ever made her any promife, and whether fhe will be marry'd to Sparkifh, or no.

Peg. Pray, dear Bud, don't, till I have fpoken with her, and told her that I have told you all ; for fhe'll kill me elfe.

Moody. Go then, and bid her come to me.

Peg. Yes, yes, Bud.

Moody. Let me fee——

Peg. I have juft got time to know of Lucy, who firft fet me to work, what lye I fhall tell next ; for I am e'en at my wits end.   [*Afide, and Exit.*

Moody. Well, I refolve it, Belville fhall have her : I'd rather give him my fifter, than lend him my wife; and fuch an alliance will prevent his pretenfions to my wife, fure—I'll make him of kin to her, and then he won't care for her.

Enter Mifs Peggy.

Peg. O Lord, Bud, I told you what anger you wou'd make me with my fifter.

Moody. Won't fhe come hither ?

Peg. No, no, fhe's afham'd to look you in the face ; fhe'll go directly to Mr. Belville, fhe fays —— She muft fpeak with him, before fhe difcovers all to you— or even fees you—She fays too, that you fhall know the reafon by-and-by—Pray let her have her way,

Bud

Bud—she won't be pacify'd if you don't—and will
never forgive me——For my part, Bud, I believe,
but don't tell any body, they have broken a piece of
filver between 'em—or have contracted one another,
as we have done, you know, which is the next thing
to being marry'd.

Moody. Pooh! you fool——she asham'd of talking with me about Belville, becaufe I made the
match for her with Sparkifh! But Sparkifh is a fool,
and I have no objection to Belville's family or fortune——tell her fo.

Peg. I will, Bud.   [*Going.*

Moody. Stay, ftay, Peggy—let her have her own
way—fhe fhall go to Belville herfelf, and I'll follow
her——that will be beft——let her have her whim.

Peg. You're in the right, Bud——for they have
certainly had a quarrel, by her crying and hanging
her head fo—I'll be hang'd if her eyes an't fwell'd
out of her head, fhe's in fuch a piteous taking.

Moody. Belville fhan't ufe her ill, I'll take care of
that—if he has made her a promife, he fhall keep to
it—but fhe had better go firft—a word or two by
themfelves will clear matters for my appearance—
will follow her at a diftance, that fhe may have no
interruption: and I will wait in the park before I fee
them, that they may come to a reconciliation before
I come upon 'em.

Peg. Law, Bud, how wife you are! I wifh I had
half your wifdom; you fee every thing at once——
Stand a one fide then—and I'll tell her you are gone
to your room, and when fhe paffes by, you may
follow her.

Moody. And fo I will—fhe fhan't fee me till I break
in upon her at Belville's.

Peg. Now for it.   [*Exit* Mifs Peggy.

Moody. My cafe is fomething better—for fuppofe
the worft—fhould Belville ufe her ill—I had rather
fight him for not marrying my fifter, than for de-
bauching my wife, for I will make her mine abfo-
lutely to-morrow; and of the two I had rather find
my fifter too forward than my wife: I expected no
other

other from her free education, as she calls it, and
her paffion for the town—Well, wife and fifter are
names which make us expect love and duty, pleafure and comfort; but we find 'em plagues and tor-
ments, and are equally, tho' differently troublefome
to their keeper. But here she comes.
[Steps on one fide.
Enter Mifs Peggy, drefs'd like Alithea; and as she
paffes over the ftage, feems to figh, fob, and wipe her
eyes.
Peg. Heigho! [Exit.
Moody. [Comes forward.] There the poor devil
goes, fighing and fobbing; a woeful example of the
fatal confequences of a town education—but I am
bound in duty, as well as inclination, to do my ut-
moft to fave her—but firft I'll fecure my own property. [Opens the door and calls.]—Peggy! Peggy!—
my dear!—I will return as foon as poffible—do you
hear me? Why don't you anfwer? You may read in
the book I bought you 'till I come back—As the
Jew fays in the play, Faft bind, faft find. [Locks the
door.] This is the beft, and only fecurity for female
affections. [Exit, holding up the key.

SCENE the park, before Belville's door.

Enter Sparkifh—fuddled.
Spark. If I can but meet with her, or any body
that belongs to her, they will find me a match for
'em—When a man has wit, and a great deal of it—
Champagne gives it a double edge, and nothing can
withftand it—'tis a lighted match to gunpowder—
the mine is fprung, and the poor devils are tofs'd
heels uppermoft in an inftant. I was right to confult
my friends, and they all agree with Moody, that I
make a damn'd ridiculous figure, as matters ftand at
prefent. I'll confult Belville—this is his houfe—he's
my friend too—and no fool—It shall be fo—damn it,
I muft not be ridiculous. [Going to the door, fees Peggy
coming.] Hold! hold! if the Champagne does not
hurt my eye-fight, while it sharpens my wit, the
enemy is marching up this way—Come on, Madam
Alithea;

Alithea; now for a fmart fire, and then let's fee who will be ridiculous.

Enter Mifs Peggy.

Peg. Dear me, I begin to tremble—there is Mr. Sparkifh, and I can't get to Mr. Belville's houfe without paffing by him—he fees me—and will difcover me—he feems in liquor too!—blefs me.

Spark. Oho! fhe ftands at bay a little—fhe don't much relifh the engagement—The firft blow is half the battle—I'll be a little figurative with her. [*Approaching her.*] I find, madam, you like a folo better than a duet. You need not have been walking alone this evening, if you had been wifer yefterday —What, nothing to fay for yourfelf?—Repentance;. I fuppofe, makes you as aukward and as foolifh, as the poor country girl your brother has lock'd up in Pall-Mall.

Peg. I'm frighten'd out of my wits.

[*Tries to pafs by him.*

Spark. Not a ftep farther fhall you go, 'till you give me an account of your behaviour, and make me reparation for being ridiculous. What, dumb ftill— then, if you won't by fair means, I muft fqueeze you to a confeffion. [*As he goes to feize her, fhe flips by him —but he catches hold of her before fhe reaches* Belville'*s door.*] Not quite fo faft, if you pleafe—Come, come, let me fee your modeft face, and hear your foft tongue—or I fhall be tempted to ufe you ill.

Enter Moody.

Moody. Hands off, you ruffian—how dare you ufe a lady, and my fifter, in this manner?

[Moody *takes her from* Sparkifh.

Spark. She's my property, fir—transferred to me by you—and tho' I would give her up to any body for a dirty fword-knot, yet I won't be bullied out of my right, tho' it is not worth that ————

[*Snaps his fingers.*

Moody. There's a fellow to be a hufband ——you are juftify'd in defpifing him, and flying from him —I'll defend you with my purfe and my fword—— knock at that door, and let me fpeak to Belville.——

2   [Peggy

[*Peggy knocks at the door, when the servant opens it, she runs it.*]—Is your mafter at home, friend?

Serv. Yes, fir.

Moody. Tell him then that I have refcu'd that lady from this gentleman, and that by her defire, and my confent, fhe flies to him for protection; if he can get a parfon, let him marry her this minute; tell him fo, and fhut the door.

Serv. And that he will, I'll anfwer for him. [*Exit.*

Spark. The man's mad, ftark mad!

Moody. And now, fir, if your wine has given you courage, you had better fhew it upon this occafion, for you are ftill damn'd ridiculous.

Spark. Did you ever hear the like!——Look ye, Mr. Moody, we are in the Park, and to draw a fword is an offence to the court—fo you may vapour as long as you pleafe. A woman of fo little tafte is not worth fighting for—fhe's not worth my fword; but if you'll fight me to-morrow morning for diverfion, I am your man.

Moody. Relinquifh your title in the lady to Belville peaceably, and you may fleep in a whole fkin.

Spark. Belville! he would not have your fifter, with the fortune of a nabob; no, no, his mouth waters at your country tid-bit at home—much good may do him.

Moody. And, you think fo, puppy—ha, ha, ha!

Spark. Yes, I do, maftiff—ha, ha, ha!

Moody. Then thy folly is complete—ha, ha, ha!

Spark. Thine will be fo, when thou haft married thy country innocence—ha, ha, ha!

[*They laugh at each other.*

Enter Harcourt.

Moody. Who have we here?

Spark. What, my boy Harcourt!

Moody. What brings you here, fir?

Harc. I follow'd you to Belville's, to prefent a near relation of yours, and a nearer one of mine, to you.

Spark. What's the matter now?

Enter

Enter a chair with Alithea.

Harc. [*Takes her by the hand.*] Give me leave, gentlemen, without offence to either, to prefent Mrs. Harcourt to you!

Spark. Alithea! your wife!——Mr. Moody, are you in the clouds too?

Moody. If I am not in a dream—I am the moft miferable waking dog, that ever run mad with his misfortunes and aftonifhment!

Harc. Why fo, Jack —can you object to my happinefs, when this gentleman was unworthy of it?

Alith. Nothing but his total indifference to me, and the higheft opinion of himfelf, could poffibly have forc'd me to fly here for protection. [*Pointing to* Harcourt, Moody *walks about in a rage.*]

Spark. This is very fine, very fine, indeed—where's your ftory about Belville now, 'fquire Moody? Prithee don't chafe and ftare, and ftride, and beat thy head, like a mad tragedy poet—but out with thy tropes and figures.

Moody. Zounds! I can't bear it.

[*Goes haftily to* Belville's *door, and knocks hard.*

Alith. Dear brother, what's the matter?

Moody. The devil's the matter! the devil and woman together. [*Knocks again.*] I'll break the door down, if they won't anfwer. [*Knocks again.*

Serv. [*At the balcony.*] What would your honour pleafe to have?

Moody. Your mafter, rafcal!

Serv. He is obeying your commands, fir, and the moment he has finifh'd, he will do himfelf the pleafure to wait on you.

Moody. You fneering villain you—if your mafter does not produce that fhe devil, who is now with him, and who, with a face of innocence, has cheated and undone me, I'll fet fire to his houfe.

[*Exit Servant.*

Spark. Gad fo! now I begin to fmoke the bufinefs. Well faid, fimplicity, rural fimplicity! Egad! if thou haft trick'd Cerberus here, I fhall be fo ravifh'd, that I will give this couple a wedding dinner. Pray, Mr. Moody, who's damn'd ridiculous now?

Moody.

Moody. [*Going to* Sparkifh.] Look ye, fir—don't grin, for if you dare to fhew your teeth at my misfortunes—I'll dafh 'em down your impudent throat, you jackanapes.

Spark. [*quite calm.*] Very fine, faith—but I have no weapons to butt with a mad bull, fo you may tofs and roar by yourfelf, if you pleafe.

Belville *appears in the balcony.*

Belv. What does my good friend want with me ?

Moody. Are you a villain, or are you not ?

Belv. I have obey'd your commands, fir.

Moody. What have you done with the girl, fir ?

Belv. Made her my wife, as you defired.

Spark. Very true, I am your witnefs—'tis pleafant, faith; ha, ha, ha! · [*Laughs to himfelf.*

Moody. She's my wife, and I demand her.

Mrs. Belville *appears in the balcony.*

Mrs. Belv. No, but I an't—What's the matter, Bud, are you angry with me ?

Moody. How dare you look me in the face, cockatrice ?

Mrs. Belv. How dare you look me in the face, Bud ? Have you not given me to another, when you ought to have married me yourfelf? Have not you pretended to be married to me, when you knew in your confcience you was not?—And have not you been fhilly-fhally for a long time? So that if I had not married. dear Mr. Belville, I fhould not have married at all—fo I fhould not.

Spark. Extremely pleafant, faith; ha, ha, ha!

Moody. I am ftupified with fhame, rage, and aftonifhment—my fate has o'ercome me—I can ftruggle no more with it. [*Sighs.*] What is left me ?—I cannot bear to look, or be look'd upon——I will hurry down to my old houfe, take a twelvemonth's provifion into it—cut down my draw-bridge, run wild about my garden, which fhall grow as wild as myfelf——then will I curfe the world, and every individual in it—and when my rage and fpirits fail me, I will be found dead among the nettles and thiftles; a woeful example of the bafenefs and treachery of one fex, and

of

of the falfehood, lying, perjury, deceit, impudence, and—damnation of the other.   [*Exit.*

[Mr. *and* Mrs. Belville *leave the balcony.*]

Spark. Very droll, and extravagantly comic, I muſt confefs ; ha, ha, ha ! [*Enter* Mr. *and* Mrs. Belville.] Look ye, Belville, I wiſh you joy, with all my heart—you have got the prize, and perhaps have caught a tartar—that's no bufinefs of mine——If you want evidence for Mr. Moody's giving his confent to your marriage, I ſhall be ready. I bear no ill-will to that pair, I wiſh you happy [*to* Mr. *and* Mrs. Harcourt.]—tho' I'm fure they'll be miferable—and fo your humble fervant.   [*Exit.*

Mrs. Belv. I hope you forgive me, Alithea, for playing your brother this trick ; indeed I ſhould have only made him and myfelf miferable, had we married together.

Alith. Then 'tis much better as it is—But I am yet in the dark how this matter has been brought about. How your innocence, my dear, has outwitted his worldly wifdom.

Belv. If you will walk in, madam, for a moment, we will tell you our adventure, and confult with you and Mr. Harcourt, the moſt likely means to reconcile your brother to us—we will be guided by you in every ſtep we take.

Alith. And we ſhall be ready and happy to effect fo defirable an end.

Mrs. Belv. I am fure I'll do any thing to pleafe my Bud but marry him.

[*She comes forward, and addreſſes the audience in the following* E P I L O G U E.

BUT you, good gentry, what fay you to this ?
You are to judge me—have I done amifs ?
I've reafons will convince you all, and ſtrong ones,
Except old folks, who hanker after young ones ;
Bud was fo paſſionate, and grown fo thrifty,
'Twas a fad life :——and then, he was near fifty !

I'll

I'm but nineteen—my husband too is young,
So soft, so gentle, such a winning tongue!
Have I, pray ladies speak, done very wrong?
As for poor Bud, 'twas honest to deceive him!
More virtuous sure, to cheat him, than to grieve him.
Great folks, I know, will call me simple slut,
Marry for love! *they cry, the country* Put!
Marriage with them's a fashion—soon grows cool:
But I'm for loving always, like a fool.
With half my fortune I would rather part,
Than be all finery, with an aching heart.
For these strange aukward notions don't abuse me;
And, as I know no better, pray excuse me.

[*Exeunt omnes.*

F I N I S.

Earl of Eſſex, by Bankes

Every Man in his Humour

Fair Penitent, by Rowe

Fair Quaker of Deal, by C. Shadwell

Falſe Friend

Fatal Curioſity

Fatal Secret, by Theobald

Flora, or Hob in the Well

Fox, by Ben Johnſon

Friendſhip in Faſhion, by Otway

Funeral, by Sir R. Steele

Gameſter, by Mrs. Centlivre

Gentle Shepherd

George Barnwell, by Lillo

Gloriana

Greenwich Park

Hamlet, by Shakeſpeare

Henry IV. 2 Parts, by ditto

Henry V. by ditto

Henry VI. 3 Parts, by ditto

Henry VIII. by ditto

Henry V. by Aaron Hill

Honeſt Yorkſhireman

Jane Gray, by Rowe

Jane Shore, by Rowe

Inconſtant, by Farquhar

King John, by Shakeſpeare

King Lear, by ditto

King Lear, by Tate

Limberham, by Dryden

Love for Love, by Congreve

Love in a Miſt

Love in a Tub, by Etherege

Love makes a Man, by C. Cibber

Love's Laſt Shift, by ditto

Lying Lover, by Steele

Macbeth, by Shakeſpeare

Man of Mode, by Etherege

Mariamne, by Fenton

Meaſure for Meaſure, by Shakeſpeare

Merchant of Venice, by Shakeſpeare

Miſtake, by Vanbrugh

Mourning Bride, by Congreve

Much ado about Nothing

Muſtapha, by Lord Orrery

Nonjuror, by C. Cibber

Oedipus, by Dryden

Old Batchelor, by Congreve

Oroonoko, by Southern

Orphan, by Otway

Othello, by Shakeſpeare

Perjured Huſband

Perolla and Iſidora, by C. Cibber

Phædra and Hippolitus, by Smith

Pilgrim, by Beaumont and Fletcher

Polly, by Mr. Gay

Propheteſs, by Beaumont

Provok'd Wife, by Vanbrugh

Recruiting Officer, by Farquhar

Refuſal, by Cibber

Rehearſal, by D. of Bucks

Relapſe, by Vanbrugh

Revenge, by Dr. Young

Richard III. by C. Cibber

Rival Fools, by C. Cibber

Rival Ladies, by Dryden

Rival Queens, by Lee

Romeo and Juliet, altered by Mr. Garrick

Royal Merchant, by Beaumont

Rule a Wife and have a Wife

School Boy, by Cibber

Scornful Lady, by Beaumont and Fletcher

She would and she would not, by Cibber

She would if she could, by Etherege

Siege of Damascus, by Hughes

Silent Woman, by B. Johnson

Sir Courtly Nice, by Crown

Sir Harry Wildair, by Farquhar

Sir Martin Mar-All, by Dryden

Sir Walter Raleigh, by Dr. Sewell

'Squire of Alfatia, by T. Shadwell

Stage Coach, by Farquhar

State of Innocence, by Dryden

Strollers

Suspicious Husband, by Dr. Hoadley

Tamerlane, by Rowe

Tempest, by Shakespeare

Tender Husband, by Steele

Theodosius, or the Force of Love

Timon of Athens, by Shakespeare

Titus and Berenice, with

the Cheats of Scapin, by Otway

Twelfth Night, by Shakespeare

Twin Rivals, by Farquhar

Two Gentlemen of Verona

Venice Preserved, by Otway

Ulysses, by Rowe

Way of the World, by Congreve

What d'ye call it? by Gay

Wife to be let

Wife's Relief, or Husband's Cure

Wild Gallant, by Dryden

Wit without Money

Woman's a Riddle

Wonder, a Woman keeps a Secret, by Centlivre

Zara, with the Interlude, by A. Hill, Esq;

Agis, 1s

Arden of Feversham, 1s

Douglas, 1s.

Eastward Hoe, 1s

Gentleman Dancing Master, 1s

Love in a Wood, 1s

Pasquin, 1s

Perkin Warbeck, 1s

Plague of Riches, French and English, 1s

Plain Dealer, 1s

Siege of Aquileia, 1s